THE LAST BEST PLACE

THE LAST BEST PLACE

Lost in the Heart of Nova Scotia

John DeMont

Doubleday Canada Limited

Canadian Cataloguing in Publication Data
DeMont, John, 1956–
    The last best place

ISBN 0-385-25604-3

1. DeMont, John, 1956–   – Journeys   – Nova Scotia.
2. Nova Scotia – Social life and customs.   3. Nova Scotia –
Description and travel.   I. Title.

FC2318.D44 1997   971.6'04   C97-930702-3
F1037.D44 1997

Cover design by Tania Craan
Cover photograph by Dan Callis
Text design by Heidy Lawrance Associates
Printed and bound in Canada

Published in Canada by
Doubleday Canada Limited
105 Bond Street
Toronto, Ontario
M5B 1Y3

The author is grateful for permission to include the following:

Excerpt from Malcolm Murray copyright M. Rankin. Reprinted by permission.

Excerpt from the diaries of Samuel de Champlain from *Gentlemen and Jesuits, Quest for Glory and Adventure in the Early Days of New France*, Elizabeth Jones, 1991, (University of Toronto Press, Toronto, Ont.) Reprinted by permission.

Excerpt from *Down North*, Ronald Caplin, editor, 1980, (Doubleday Canada Limited, Toronto, Ont.) Reprinted by permission.

Excerpt from correspondences between Adelaide Kuntz and Marsden Hartley and excerpt from *Cleophas and His Own* by Marsden Hartley, The Yale Collection of American Literature, Beinecke Rare Book and Manuscript Library, Yale University. Reprinted by permission.

To Lisa, Belle and Sam

CONTENTS

ACKNOWLEDGEMENTS

This is a book about home, specifically my own, which is the province of Nova Scotia. I'm indebted to countless people for their hospitality, time and stories. If they'll have it, this book is theirs. Any shortcomings on the other hand, are mine. That this book came about at all is due in large part to the guidance and determination of John Pearce, the wisdom and judgement of Charis Wahl and the precise pen of Shaun Oakey. They are the best of editors. Most of all I want to thank Lisa Napier, my first editor and ever-present sounding board. She, more than anyone, kept this book moving forward when at times it seemed to be standing still.

He had been walking around Halifax all day, as though by moving through familiar streets he could test whether he belonged here and had at last reached home.

Hugh MacLennan

—

Preface

Panic. I am headed for the end of the line. And Lord, I have made a mistake. Not necessarily a big mistake, like kicking Conrad Black's schnauzer. But a mistake, nevertheless. Lisa is coming later on a bigger plane. I had conveniently forgotten about the puddle-hopper aircraft that take off no matter what the weather, bound for postage-stamp Maritime runways shrouded in fog and sleet, buffeted by angry winds that strike from crazy angles. My stomach is raked by razor blades; the walls close in like a coffin. *Think of an airplane as an unsinkable cork in the ocean*, I recall reading in one of those cure-yourself-of-fear-of-flying articles. *Scotch!* my soul cries as I lean into the aisle, shooting panicky glances in search of the drinks trolley.

Ten minutes later we break through to blue sky. I am alive. My reflection in the window bears the blissed-out, beatific appearance of someone bound for a Tony Robbins convention. I even smile with uncharacteristic benevolence at the plumber from Cape Breton seated next to me. His face has a reddish hue that glows brighter with each mini-bottle of Grand Marnier. On his last flight, he has already confided without the least embarrassment, he was caught smoking in the men's can and thrown off in Montreal. I'm thumbing through an Elmore Leonard paperback as he tells me this. So when he makes a fumbling swipe at the flight attendant's butt I seriously consider giving the suckah a rabbit punch to the bridge of the nose. But she cowed him with a single look, leaving me to return to contemplating the clouds.

Because only from the air do you really understand that you've gone as far on this continent as a person can go. Only from thirty thousand feet do you really sense just how tenuous the connection to the mainland is—a thin band of land. Otherwise Nova Scotia is an island, in spirit as well as geography. Ahead, I knew, lay highlands and valleys, rivers that meandered in gentle loops, and a nasty, pounding ocean that made widows of young fishermen's wives. Ahead was a place where the premier bayed like a dog in the legislature, where Roman Catholic priests married the ex-wives of media tycoons, and Tibetan holy men found the promised land. Ahead was music floating from red-neck taverns and black revivalist churches, from Legions and kitchens. Ahead lay blueberries, Christmas trees, lighthouses, lobsters and strange accents that mingle Scotland, Ireland, Britain, France, Germany and America. Ahead lay the crossroads where the warm Gulf Stream encounters the numbing Labrador Current, the plants of the High Arctic intermingle with the animals of Louisiana. Ahead, I felt certain in my heart, lay something elemental and true, something fundamentally different and essentially better than what I was leaving.

At least this was the jumble of romantic images I held as myth-laden truth, like tribal paintings on a cave wall.

"Where ya from, buddy?" asks my seatmate, now cut off from Air Canada's liquor supply.

That's a question you hear a lot from Nova Scotians. I've heard them ask it in Whitehorse, in Ottawa, in Calgary, Toronto, Boston, on the Isle of Skye and even from a small town in Norway. Note the arched eyebrows, the inflection, the emphasis on the word *from*. They are important. As casual as the words sound, there is nothing idle in the question. What they are trying to do is place you on their geographic and psychic landscape. *Who are your people?* they really want to know. *Are you one of us?* The code is as well established as Masonic ritual.

Nova Scotians living away refer to that far-off place as "Down Home." Unless we've been drinking, we don't try to tell others because they just wouldn't understand. We babble about the low crime, clean water and reasonable housing prices—sounding like a flack for the local chamber of commerce—and say that the lifestyle is what brings us back. Ultimately, there is little to be gained in letting others know that Nova Scotians, more than most people, believe that in roots can be found character. That out on the margins a need exists to be anchored to the dead and to locate your identity in time. Your past and your people are always with you. So, it seems, is being born here.

We are not totally naive. We realize we're all wanderers and vagabonds; we're all from everywhere; we all write our own lives as we go along. And yet, and yet. Something compels us to jump off the corporate ladder to open up a candlemaking shop in some burp of a place that doesn't see as much traffic in a year as a Yorkville boutique in a single afternoon. Something makes us pack the family and drive like wild-eyed maniacs for eighteen straight hours to swim in water not fit for warm-blooded mammals. Something causes us to gather over rum-and-Cokes in kitchens at parties in Lloydminster or Kamloops or Sudbury and brood about things hundreds of miles away.

This is beyond family, myth and memory. I have a theory. It sounds a little New Agey but here goes anyway: each of us has only one right place where we would rather shiver in the rain than lounge in the sunshine anywhere else; maybe where we would rather die than live anywhere else. It is about where you belong, not necessarily where you were born or where your family live. *Home*, the idea as much as the molecules of a place. Where the heart is, or isn't, where they have to take you in, where you can never go back. Home that is born in you, follows you and makes you who you are. That consumes you as you consume it. That you can never escape. Home, where you belong no matter how much its face changes.

My hypothesis is that each of us spends our life searching for our own Last Best Place. The ones who find it, the lucky ones, the connected ones, do not all live in physical proximity to their special place: the exiled Italian restaurant workers, tailors and tile and terrazzo artisans who gather around espressos in the deep bowels of North American cities to gossip about their home towns; the bank executive from Boston who returns to his beloved Ireland each summer and plans to retire there; the Canadian journalists, diplomats and stockbrokers who make their way to the only skating rink in all of London lined the right way for hockey. But even when I was among the temporarily displaced I knew it could be far worse. Those who never find home—who are never even sure what they are looking for—are doomed to endless wandering, moving from town to town constantly searching for that one place that will give them context. They have no choice; it is human nature to strive for connection and spiritual nourishment. The search can take anyone anywhere. It has taken me back home to Nova Scotia.

The Mi'kmaqs, of course, were always here. Europeans followed—first perhaps Viking adventurers in the Dark Ages, then hardy Basque and Breton fishermen. Tradition says that John Cabot landed on Cape Breton Island in 1497 and there he refilled his water casks from a tumbling stream. Before long European fishermen were heading each spring to the Grand Banks near Newfoundland and the waters near Acadia—a territory that included, roughly, the present-day Maritime provinces as well as northern New England—so called because when Giovanni da Verrazano explored the area in 1524 its beauty and richness reminded him of tales of Arcadia, a region of ancient Greece celebrated by poets as a pastoral paradise. Eventually, the French tried the land, grudgingly, lest their English rivals beat them to it. At the turn of the seventeenth century the seriously deluded Marquis de la Roche dreamed of a settlement on Sable Island, an inhospitable, treeless spit of land two hundred miles from the mainland. He dropped sixty French convicts there, then forgot about them. When someone finally came to rescue them three years later, only eleven still lived, the rest lying buried in a small sand plot.

Life here has never been easy—about what you would expect of a place born of ill-advised colonial ambition, dependent for its very existence on a sea that swallows sailors and fishermen of all nations with terrible equanimity. The French did finally hack lives out of the wilderness. The English followed, scattering Germans, Swiss and the Dutch to counteract the French presence and, they hoped, to wean the Acadians from their ancient Catholic faith. When that failed they herded the French onto ships and resettled them in English colonies to the south, leaving the land for the Lowlands Scots and the farmers, fishermen and merchants of New England to gobble up. Next came the Loyalists from the rebel American colonies and thousands of Highlanders, dispersed by the Clearances.

The miracle, I always felt, was that so many stayed. Who can blame the ones who took one look at the frightening mass of trees that ran right down to the icy water, raked a hand through the lumpy, rock-filled soil, considered the stories of the bloodthirsty savages waiting in the wilderness and kept on going right down to New England? By the end of the nineteenth century the ambitious, the adventurous and the young were gone. The mines and shipyards had closed. The forests had reclaimed the once-cleared land.

Abandoned farms and homesteads rotted in the damp. You can see them everywhere still, the fallen-in cellars and decrepit apple trees that mark these lost dreams.

That left us.

For against all odds, somehow the place hung on. Despite its doomed economy, in spite of being out there on the edge of the continent, people came, built families, homes and businesses, fought, attended church and went spectacularly mad. My people are the French, Scottish and English yeomanry of smalltown Nova Scotia. We are a tribe of miners, teachers, musicians, athletes, housewives, lawyers, janitors and businessmen. We are Baptists and whisky drinkers, of high morals and low cunning. We are men and women named McKeigan, Briers, Brown, Lamond and Levy whose names can now be found on tombstones in places called Glace Bay, Sydney Mines, Windsor, Halifax and Chester Basin. My realization that Nova Scotia is fundamentally different from everywhere else came a week after my wedding, when Lisa and I headed down the road to Calgary, where bumper stickers read "Let the Eastern bastards freeze in the dark" and where a mayor with a gut like a sumo champ raised his popularity a couple of points by bleating about how Maritimers on the dole were raising the crime rate in his city.

Let the fat man talk. Calgary and then Toronto made me Nova Scotian in a way that I would not have been had I not left. Cringe to think about the way I stood around at parties, this mystical, far-away look in my eye like King Arthur reminiscing about Camelot as I went on about my home. I defended the dubious honour of Nova Scotia's politicians as each successive scandal hit the national press. I lit into a slack-jowled paper pusher from soulless Etobicoke who spent an expense-account lunch droning on about "the lack of a Maritime work ethic." I actually found myself standing at a bar late one night before a woman with three nose rings, extolling the virtues of Rita MacNeil. *Rita MacNeil!*

Then I realized something essential: *that* (Nova Scotia) was still home and *this* (Calgary and Toronto) still away. And thus it would always be, even if I couldn't articulate why. I knew that Nova Scotia was in some respects the perfect fantasy spot. There's the inspiring geography for starters, the highlands, the valleys, the jigsaw coastline and preternaturally powerful tides. There's also the matter of being at the end of the line, something about the endless, mystical promise of the ocean and of being precariously balanced between the New World and the Old. Some people are just drawn to places where life is close to the edge and to the elements. So along with the sober and the ambitious, the place attracted the losers and misfits with nowhere else to run, the crazed dreamers with ideas too big for more conventional places, the obsessed romantics convinced that they've finally found truth.

Is it any surprise that people and things are just a little out of whack here? In Nova Scotia horses live in bungalow basements, barroom drunks sleep standing up, motorcycle riders use socks for gloves. I know of a man who keeps his casket and tombstone in the living room and his favourite cat in the deep-freeze. Let's face it, any place that can accommodate the same French stock that spawned the Ragin' Cajuns of Louisiana, wild-eyed Scottish Highlanders and stubborn Loyalists who preferred allegiance to the British crown to independence is big enough to ensure that fantasies never wear out. Even the Gaelic name, New Scotland, seems to extend back into a distant romantic haze.

My Nova Scotia, when I thought about it truthfully, was less an entity than an abstraction. I knew that a whole big world and all the good jobs were elsewhere. I just needed the *concept* of Nova Scotia out there on the horizon, in case everything went to ratshit. Except now I was on this plane heading back to Nova Scotia terrified that reality would spoil the memory forever. That the whole concept was no more than a fiction of a feverishly wistful imagination. That you can't go home again.

I knew that so much *hadn't* changed since we left. Province House still seemed to be run by crooks. Miners, fishermen and steelworkers were still facing extinction as their industries died and the flood of federal money that kept the place afloat was inexorably drying up. But in my absence the province had become a demographic paradox: a place whose population is essentially stable yet seems suddenly to consist mostly of people who were born elsewhere. On any day in Nova Scotia a traveller might encounter a Hollywood actor, an old Haight-Ashbury flower child, an adventurer from Ceylon, a novelist from Ireland, an avant-garde composer from New York, the world's strongest man or a holy man from Nepal. Where did all these Germans come from? What about these

Buddhists everywhere? Who were these downshifters, back-to-the-landers, spiritual seekers who opened restaurants that used cloth napkins and flogged software to Silicon Valley while looking out on the Bay of Fundy? Who were these people who overpaid for exposed headlands where the winter westerlies got up to 100 mph and the waves wore away a foot of shoreline a year? What was going through their minds when they started up cosy, doomed bed-and-breakfasts in neglected corners of Cape Breton and the Annapolis Valley?

I sort of understood. For people like these, Nova Scotia meant wide-open spaces when most people live in cramped communities. It suggested freedom from dirt, crime and urban blight. It still resonates with a haunting echo of the past when pockets of this ageing continent were still virginal. Had the dreamers, the terminally deranged, the spiritual seekers and every hippy still in captivity found something more important? Did Nova Scotia somehow fulfil the yearning of the times? Had they found their special place here on the end of the continent?

At this point, I really had no idea. All I could do was speak for myself. Which I did by turning to the drunken plumber beside me and saying, "From Nova Scotia."

"Ah," he sighed, flopping back in his chair. "Then you're going home too."

PART ONE

Dreams, Legends and the Meaning of Land

*There was a strange sound of stillness
about it all. As if the pine needles and
the dead leaves and the grey rocks
and the clean-smelling brook
with the pole bridge they
passed over were all singing
together a quiet song,
like the drowsy hum
of wires or of bees.*

Ernest Buckler

———

One

The Cosmic G-Spot

—

THIS IS A BOOK ABOUT A CONCEPT THAT ORIGINATES IN THE SOUL, SO I DON'T want you to be put off by ancient rocks and hard, barren soil, mountains that stretch into the sky and mines that bore deep into the ground, unbroken forest that pushes right down to the shore and an ocean that gives everything its taste, smell, feel, language and heart. Nova Scotia is an elemental place of soft, heartbreaking beauty, but there is nothing fundamentally gentle about it: people still die when fireballs shoot through mine shafts and fishing trawlers go down in winter hurricanes. You can't ignore waves that wipe out entire waterfronts or tides that lift fishing boats from the sea-floor mud like the hands of invisible giants. The world is wilder here, more dangerous and bitter, more extravagant and bright. It shapes the people as only savage, magnificent places do. Home, then, is landscape—the architecture and ambiance of life. And that, therefore, is where we shall start.

Nova Scotia, if there is any justice, ought to be seen first from the sea. We should all be like old-time Basque fishermen high on the mast scanning the horizon as it disappears from view behind each passing swell for our first glimpse of the highlands of Cape Breton, say, or the great harbour at the place the Mi'kmaqs called Chebucto. Mostly now you see it by air, heading east from some more important spot towards Halifax, which is what Chebucto is now called. Romantics like to think the province is shaped like a lobster. I've always felt it looked like a prehistoric bird, the ugly, predatory kind with a name fifteen letters long that died out couple of hundred million years ago. But maybe the best way to picture Nova Scotia is to picture Britain. Shrink it down, strip it of people. What is similar is the land: wild and mountainous in the north, the central parts shot through with the same veins of coal; everywhere good harbours providing shelter for cities and towns built along the same ocean. Nova Scotia is centuries younger than Britain, but for North America it is a doddering, ancient place. And both are damp—as likely to be foggy as raining—populated out of necessity by tea sippers and spirit swillers forever trying to drive the chill from their joints.

The parallels are not accidental. Until 300 million years ago Nova Scotia lay near the equator deep inside a seamless supercontinent beside what would become the Cornwall coast of England. A hundred million years later the supercontinent began to split into the continents of Africa, Europe and North and South America. The main rupture finally came just east of Nova Scotia, the cosmic G-spot.

At ground level you know why Henry Wadsworth Longfellow wrote "This is the forest primeval" in *Evangeline*, his poem about

Nova Scotia. But from the air you're struck by how close the province is to being submerged: surrounded by ocean, dotted by lakes, segmented by rivers. Nowhere are you more than an hour's drive from the sea. Three-quarters of the population lives within five miles of the ocean. The coastline weaves and rolls, juts and twists. Time hasn't done much to smooth Nova Scotia's sharp, prehistoric edges, more than 6,000 miles of them, a coast longer than the breadth of the entire continent.

I've travelled the next-best thing—all the existing highways and byways. Which means I have been truly blessed. Even on the most agonizingly dull section of Nova Scotia road—the section where you've got the windows down, head stuck out like a basset hound, gulping air to stay awake—a weird scene will cross your windshield and give you a jolt. You cannot, for example, drive for half an hour in any direction without passing a warning from some fringe band of religious zealots that The End Is Upon Us, a hunk of some unnameable, nasty-looking roadkill, or the remnants of a blown-out tire, which always, to my mind, hints at something truly awful. The abandoned roadside footwear has always given me pause: the pair of sneakers beneath the overpass, the tasseled loafer in the gutter, the black rubber boot on the broken yellow line.

As for the passing parade of humans, well, Frederico Fellini wouldn't have to give casting calls in Nova Scotia. Just get behind the wheel, hit the road and say, "You, you, you, you're all hired." Not long ago on the outskirts of Halifax I saw a mad man in a good suit sitting on the grass island between the divided highway babbling cheerfully in the burning midafternoon sun. Once someone in a Halloween mask driving a rusty Cadillac played chicken with me for nearly twenty miles east from Yarmouth before flipping me the bird and driving off. Once I spent a sweaty half hour as the lone male in a car full of women behind a bunch of Hells Angels who slowed to a crawl and gestured jacking off until they got bored— at least I hope that's what made them stop—and roared off.

In Nova Scotia instead of the landscape being a backdrop to the daily pulse of life it's the other way around. Hit the road and you realize this implicitly. Go west, say, from Halifax. Past Herring Cove and Portuguese Cove, Ketch Harbour, Cape Sambro, Pennant, Terence Bay, Prospect and Shad Bay. Beyond East Dover, West Dover, Peggy's Cove, Indian Harbour and Seabright. Through Queensland and Hubbards, Bayswater and Blandford. Past the chi-chi new homes of the stockbrokers, developers and doctors who commute to Halifax and past the sturdy wooden jobs built a century ago by prosperous lobster fishermen. Drive by the shop of John Little the blacksmith, who composes jazz on his forge and reconstructs dinosaur skeletons in New York museums, and the place where Elisabeth Mann Borgese, the daughter of Thomas Mann, lives with her special citations from the United Nations for her work helping to save the world's oceans, and with the Irish setters she's taught to type and play the piano.

Then you reach Mahone Bay. Shift your gaze seaward to the tufted islands, which have been there since the Ice Age, when glacial till was moulded by the moving ice into oval hills called drumlins.

Nova Scotia has 4,500 islands, which may be the largest proliferation in the smallest space anywhere in the world. A waitress at the Chester Yacht Club once told me that Mahone Bay had 365, "one for each day of the year." But the truth is there are about seventy-five if you count every rock. I enjoy the names, like Big Duck, Little Fish, Mark, Lynch, Mountain, Saddle, Snake, Graves, Flat, Quaker, Meiseners, Clay, Birch, Grassy, Frog, Sand, Ironbound, Mason, Rafuse, Star, Woody, Love, Round and Marvins. Most of all I enjoy just looking at them, because like most people I have a thing for islands. They can be pretty or dramatic. They are perfect metaphors—"no man is an island," "the island within." And fantasies, from a twelfth-dynasty Egyptian story about a castaway and Plato's account of Atlantis to every soft-porn movie going.

Tides also have a way of capturing the imagination. You realize this after making the big turn up around Digby Neck into the Bay of Fundy. These are waters than turn back muscular river currents and form waves for joyriders to crest. They are, in the truest sense, a genuine wonder. Regular as clockwork, twice every twenty-four hours and fifty minutes, 100 billion tons of water—as much as the entire Gulf Stream, two thousand times the St. Lawrence—pour into this 200-million-year-old rift valley cradled between Nova Scotia and New Brunswick. It is a funnel really, seventy-five miles wide between Yarmouth and Maine, narrowing to a mere twenty-eight at Cape Chignecto. Near there the world's highest tides—rising and falling more than fifty feet during spring—occur when the sun and moon are aligned to exert maximum pull on the earth's waters.

I got this last bit of information from Harry Thurston's superb book *Tidal Life*. It is an immense help to me because I do not live in a Newtonian world. Cause and effect means about the same to me as the thought of God sitting on a mountaintop somewhere. I have no idea who turned on the lights. Or why. I look at the fishing boats stuck in the mud, drive by again a few hours later when they bob in a nice chop over exactly the same spot and think "Well, would ya look at that," then stumble towards the next miracle. In this case, the Wind Birds, a million or so migrating sandpipers, that each summer descend on Fundy like a cloud, banking, gliding and twisting but never colliding in their ever-changing patterns. They descend on the mud flats, grazing on the thousands of sand shrimp that live in the muck—their last meal before the final leg of the journey to the north coast of South America.

Wonders abound at the end of Fundy, at the base of the thin isthmus that connects the province to the rest of the continent, where the world's greatest tides have stripped away 200 million years' worth of land until the cliffs shimmer with the layers of geologic time, like a serving of spumoni ice cream. Welcome to Nova Scotia's Jurassic Park: 150 years ago the remains of the first terrestrial reptile ever discovered were found in the fossil tree trunks here; in 1986 a team of American scientists uncovered the biggest dinosaur fossil find in North America along the shores of Fundy.

Around here is a village called Parrsboro and the Parrsboro Rock & Mineral Shop. The place was packed last time I stopped in, which was about 5:30 p.m. I perused the fossils and fondled the fancy rocks that glittered like candy. I kept stalling because I wanted to talk to the proprietor, who was busy working the room, basking in his peculiar fame. Eldon George is a lot sharper than he looks, standing there in a tractor-dealership hat, snap-buttoned checked shirt and jeans. When I finally got him to myself he explained how he turned to rockhounding at the age of eight after a fall from a barn rafter fractured his arm in eight places and left him with atrophied muscles, a drop wrist and no future as an athlete, his first career choice.

Then he told me what I took to be his favourite story. "It was April 10, 1984, and I was exploring in the cliffs around Parrsboro. It started to get cold so I stepped behind a cliff and saw a mysterious shape in the red sand at my feet. All of a sudden I wasn't cold any more," he said, gesturing with his good arm at the slab of rock in the glass case, pale sandstone, criss-crossed with tiny, perfectly preserved three-toed prints. Nearby were pewter copies of the little tracks. I picked one up. On the back was printed, "World's smallest dinosaur track. Found by Eldon George."

The tides do strange things. For long stretches the land in the Bay of Fundy goes flat with acre after acre of salt marshes and bogs built from deposits laid down by the high tides. Then steep cliffs and strange formations carved out by the surging water. The Mi'kmaqs felt it a holy place; Glooscap, their giant man-spirit, was said to owe his power to Cape Blomidon. I cannot say. The only time I tried to hike Cape Split, a four-mile headland stretching out into the Minas Basin, we somehow missed the turn for the trail altogether and plunged immediately into deep, hilly woods, forging ahead dumbly. All we had was a big thermos of Tim Horton's coffee and a quart of rum, which we pulled on with the grim single-mindedness of escaped convicts. At points we were reduced to hauling ourselves on tree roots up perpendicular hills. I stepped over a fallen tree, slipped and slid down a hill head-first like Pete Rose taking second. We sang songs as we plunged ahead, quickly learned that none of us knew the same lyrics and were left to repeat the chorus to "Chain Gang" (*uhhhh, ahhhhh, uhhhh, ahhhh, uhhhh ahhhh, ohohohoh, uhhhh ahhhh*) until we burst through the woods into the parking lot where our girlfriends, who had been to the top of the cape and back, sat in the car dead asleep.

There are so many spots where the land meets the water that sure seem like holy places. Even someone with a spirit as earth-bound as mine feels touched by grace climbing Cape Breton's famed Cabot Trail. I'm convinced everyone on Earth must know this view, even if just subconsciously. Or maybe it just seems like every time I flip open a magazine or change channels there's the same wonderful combination of mountains, sea, sky, forest and road helping to flog some new beer or the latest-model Nissan on the lots. Partway up to the summit there's a place to stop. Everything and everyone is quiet. From this angle, the world seems wider, more worthy of terror and celebration. I know you can't take it with you. But a place like here makes you think that maybe there's no need. Perspective is liberating. Looking at a view like this, you know you're an ant, a blade of grass. Your shoulders start to relax.

There's nothing to be done. So just ignore it, or see. Then start the curving, zig-zag descent, so sudden that you do it in second gear, brake pushed to the floor, the smell of smouldering rubber filling your nostrils.

When they recede the tides leave strange things washed up on the beaches: half-billion-dollar bales of pot, confused whales, half-dead boat people, fishermen who never learned to swim, drinkers—their faces frozen in surprise—who fell out of their powerboats when someone hit the clutch while they were taking a leak. A century ago two fishermen came upon a legless man on a beach near Digby, on the Bay of Fundy, using his stumps and the heels of his palms to propel himself towards the surf, presumably to drown. They restrained him and got him to shelter. But the stranger couldn't or wouldn't say anything when asked what happened to his legs, other than the words "Jerome," "Columbo" and "*fretto*" (Italian for frozen). A theory did circulate that he was an Italian stowaway who had jumped ship in New Brunswick, working at odd jobs in a lumber camp near Saint John, until he got lost in the woods, soaked himself to the knees and had to have his legs amputated. The people of Saint John, the story went, looked after him for a while. When he got too expensive they hired some American sailors to ship him across the Bay of Fundy and dump him on a beach. Jerome never confirmed the story. He never said much of anything, really, before he died in 1912. He was a grumpy bastard, prone to lashing out at people for no reason. But the folk at Sandy Cove, N.S., looked after him anyway, giving him a place to stay in a fisherman's home and allotting him two dollars a week for living expenses.

At times the retreating tides seemed to leave beaches covered with death. From land it's impossible to see Sable Island, where the Elizabethan nobleman Sir Humphrey Gilbert's ship *Delight* broke up in 1583. But so many sailing ships, steamers and modern freighters have gone down on the island's shoals and sandbars that it has more than earned its heart-warming nickname of the Graveyard of the Atlantic. Brier Island, the small headland in the approach to the Bay of Fundy, is the Graveyard of Fundy. With its rough waters and craggy ledges this is a treacherous spot, whether shrouded by fog in summer or swirling in snow in winter. During the fairly typical winter of 1846, of the twenty-five vessels carrying lumber through the bay that season only nine made it. The disasters for the shipowners and passengers were considered God's bountiful harvest to islanders. Salvaged lumber built the Odd Fellows' Hall in Westport, the island's only village. On Brier they still talk about wreckers who used lanterns to lure rumrunners, warships, steamers and passenger ships onto its shoals and ledges for profit.

Yarmouth County is another spot cursed by sea captains, shipowners and the marine insurers back at Lloyd's of London. From 1831 to 1902, no fewer than 133 sailing vessels and steamers were wrecked there. The fate of the *City of Monticello* was not unusual. A 232-foot passenger steamer, she foundered one day near the turn of the century within sight of the town of Yarmouth's widow's walks. Only four of the forty men aboard made it to safety before she rolled over and sank, taking the lifeboats down with her. And the corpses floated ashore at nearby Cheboque Point.

Even in the late days of the twentieth century chaos and menace are never far from life. Which is why we have names. To name something is to take control of it. Especially in Nova Scotia, where living means a particular way of being in a landscape, of coexisting with land and sea. In a compartment on the driver's door in my car I keep a map. Nothing special, just a provincial Department of Tourism model. It's battle scarred: coffee and pizza stains, some notes in my indecipherable scrawl, a big chunk ripped out of one corner. But it is an eternal joy to read. Look at the wonky beauty of names like Ecum Secum, Main-à-Dieu, Eskasoni, Ben Eoin, Shubenacadie, Malagash, Tatamagouche, Mushaboom and Mabou. The portent of the Hawk, Wreck Cove, Black Rock, Chapel Island, Murder Island, Devil's Island, Roaring Bull Point and Malignant Cove. The romance of Martinique, White Capes and MacNeils Vale. The plain strangeness of Ass Point, Neck Pond, Eyeball Run and Mira Gut.

Often the naming is obvious: an act of ownership as in Copeland Bog, a warning as in Squally Point. Many times there's no logic, none at all. It seems totally whimsical. One minute you're driving down the South Shore, the next, for no discernible reason, you're on the Western Shore. And why, within a couple of miles, do you weave through Lower West Pubnico, Middle West Pubnico, West

Pubnico, Lower East Pubnico, Middle East Pubnico, Centre East Pubnico, East Pubnico, Pubnico Point and plain old Pubnico? Between the nine of them there must be, let's see, all of three hundred people.

Maybe it is understandable that there might be a Balls Creek, a Three Fathom Harbour or a Four Mile Brook. But does there also have to be a Rear Balls Creek, a Lower Three Fathom Harbour and a Six Mile Brook? Except perhaps that a certain immutable law is at work here: naming these places, no matter how microscopic, literally puts them on the map. Only then, on a certain level, do the people who live there exist.

Two

Laughter in the Wind

—

I GREW UP LIKE MOST PEOPLE IN NOVA SCOTIA: UNCONSCIOUSLY BREATHING the air of history. We knew only fragments of the story—even if we had a sense that another dimension existed here, a reservoir of fact and myth that extended beyond the boundaries of mere matter.

Odd facts and stories were what stuck in our young minds: we knew about the stunted ponies that lived on Sable Island; we knew about Giant MacAskill, the strongman from Cape Breton, who died after imbedding a ship's anchor in his shoulder while performing one of his amazing feats of strength; we knew that each year Halifax sent a great Christmas tree to Boston for the help it lent after the Halifax Explosion, the world's largest before the atom bomb.

We knew that once the coal fields of Pictou County and Cape Breton had carried the province. And that long before today's long flat line of economic stagnation—begun by Confederation and the trade policies that helped Central Canada while devastating the Maritimes—Nova Scotia had been a prosperous, self-sufficient crown colony with an economy built on the Golden Age of Sail. That there had been privateers and raiding parties that emerged from the fog and burned and looted the villages and settlements.

That there had been the ragged smugglers and pirates and hon-oured sea captains and boat builders. We knew that it had been the gateway to the continent, through which half the country seemed to have passed. We knew about wars and treaties and great rivalries and the great fortress of Louisbourg, which held the key to the con-tinent. And we knew all about the pioneers, those baffled opti-mists, those hard-scrabble poor coming from nowhere to never-been, who stared out with awe, relief, dread and devotion from the decks as they made for harbour and this new place.

This was the history that shaped the land and the people. Nova Scotia cannot be measured by width and breadth. It has a third dimension: time. It is top-heavy with history. And if we did not have it committed to memory it was only because here the past so over-lays the present that history is vibrant and alive. Children crave places like this, where heroes battle, time is jumbled together and little ships discover new places on the edge of the new creation. The house I grew up in was as old as the city of Calgary. In Nova Scotia time travel is still easy because progress hasn't paved over the artifacts and ghosts. History lives on here, always tinged with that special melancholy—looking longingly forward or achingly back—that gives it the power to haunt.

It is overcast, low twenties with a nice breeze as Lisa, our four-year-old, Belle, newborn Sam and I circle the Annapolis Basin towards Port Royal. All I can think about is what a wonderful people Canadians really are. Don't scoff. To get to Port Royal take an extension off Highway 101 through a valley, past the herb farms, the galleries and the nice bed-and-breakfasts. I zip by Auberge sieur de Monts and the Champlain Motel. This is the cradle of Canada, for the entire continent. The place where it all started, as some local tourism bumf points out, "two years before the first permanent English settlement at Jamestown, Virginia, three years before the founding of Quebec, and fifteen years before the Pilgrims landed at Plymouth, Massachusetts." Imagine if this were in the States. The road would be lined with DeMont's Donuts, Champlain's Exotic Dancing Palace, Marc Lescarbot's Liquor and Firearm Emporium and crummy little curio shops selling Port Royal ashtrays. There would be a wax museum, the kind where every figure resembles Prince Charles, and a tacky playhouse where crack addicts and convicted junk bond dealers in period costume go on about the virtues of self-reliance and the capitalist system.

Instead, the Canadian government used a sketch Samuel de Champlain made of the layout of the original settlement to build a terrific replica on the site. I am way overdue here. No one on my father's side of the family is actually certain how long people named DeMont have been around this province. But that small detail has never stopped us from claiming descendance from the Huguenot nobleman Pierre du Gua, sieur de Monts, who was given the original charter to settle "the countries, territories, coasts and confines of La Cadie ... from the 40th degree unto the 46th." Which, if I'm not mistaken, makes him North America's first franchisee.

He attracted the normal crew of downtrodden losers, deluded

adventurers and desperate strivers. There were masons and carpenters to clear the wilderness, interpreters to trade with the Indians, a few wild-eyed clerics to add to the converted, a scattering of gentlemen on the long downwards skid through French society. Towering over everyone was Jean de Biencourt, generally known as sieur de Poutrincourt, who fought on both sides of France's religious wars and now, at forty-seven, was ready to start life over again, uprooting his wife and family from their seigneuries in Picardy and Champagne in the hope of adventure, honour and wealth. Penniless and embroiled in a snake's nest of lawsuits back in France, he had the vaulting ambition of the privileged come down in the world. No little cabin in the woods for him. He envisioned a French domain—handsome manor houses surrounded by smiling fields and pastures, church bells ringing out, "the tawny skinned inhabitants," as Elizabeth Jones wrote in her book *Gentlemen and Jesuits: Quests for Glory and Adventure in the Early Days of New France,* "emerging devoutly from their wigwams to pray."

They were at sea for two months in 1604, riding out brutal storms and a close call with icebergs. Then they saw here. Champlain, a soldier, sailor, writer, mapmaker and adventurer—a big-spirited renaissance man—called it "one of the finest harbours I have ever seen on all these coasts where a couple of thousand vessels could lie in safety." But no doubt it was de Monts's call. Prefiguring centuries of ill-fated family investment decisions, my alleged ancestor chose to settle on a godforsaken island on the

New Brunswick side of the Bay. The clouds of blackflies puffed the men's faces up like soufflés. The cider froze and had to be hacked out of an icy amber block and weighed by the pound; the settlers took to drinking old dirty water and melted snow. Before long some of them began to feel their gums swell and the flesh thicken in their mouths. Champlain, the meticulous note-taker, gave a detailed account of what happened as the scurvy progressed:

> There was engendered in the mouths of those who had it large pieces of superfluous flesh (which caused a great putrefaction) and this increased to such a degree that they could scarcely take anything except in very liquid form. Their teeth barely held in their place, and could be drawn out with the fingers without causing pain. This superfluous flesh was often cut away, which caused them to lose much blood from the mouth. Afterwards, they were taken with great pains in the arms and legs, which became swollen and very hard and covered with spots like flea-bites; and they could not walk on account of the contraction of the nerves; consequently they had almost no strength, and suffered intolerable pains. They had also pains in the lines, stomach, and bowels, together with a very bad cough and shortness of breath. In brief, they were in such a state that the majority of the sick could neither get up nor move, nor could they even be held upright without fainting away.

You get the picture. Come winter break-up the survivors couldn't get out of there fast enough. They beat it back across the basin, through Digby Gut to a spot with lots of trees for firewood, streams for water and hills for windbreak. There they founded North America.

I do feel a twinge of ancestral pride as I walk towards the log walls of Port Royal. I fantasize that the Parks Canada woman at the visitors gate takes one look at my face, notices the familial resemblance and lets me in for free. But I pay up, walk down the dirt driveway and around the outside of the fort for a while. I inspect the statue of Christ on the tall wooden cross standing in the mowed field marking the cemetery for the scurvy victims. I look at the woods from where first walked Membertou, the great Mi'kmaq sagamo—said to be over a hundred years old and described by one of the settlers as being "of prodigious size, and taller and stronger than most, bearded like a Frenchman while not one of the others had hair on his chin." Then I step inside.

Lord, it is tiny: the storehouse, the chapel, the kitchen, the blacksmith shop, the small, modestly furnished gentlemen's quarters all forming a rectangle around a central courtyard. The plan was sixteenth-century manoral Normandy. But it is all not much bigger than a suburban monster home in Etobicoke. Icy wind whistled through the cracks in the walls; unknown devilish terrors lurked in the woods and the waters, and the aristocrats back in Versailles wanted to pull the plug on the whole thing.

But I've always had a warmer, happier image of life in Port Royal.

I picture Champlain and the others returning from a voyage of exploration in November 1606 to find costumed colonists and Indians in canoes beginning the first performance of *Le Théâtre de Neptune en la Nouvelle-France,* a play in verse written by Marc Lescarbot, the lawyer and dreamer for the occasion. And the Ordre de Bon Temps, the continent's first dining club, designed to keep the troops healthy, happy and mutiny-free during the deep freeze. The chief steward leading off with a napkin over his shoulder, a special chain of office around his neck and a staff in his hand, the others following, each carrying a dish, which they placed with due formality upon the long high table set with gleaming pewter before a great stone fireplace. There sat the other gentlemen, Membertou and the other visiting Indian chiefs. The role of steward for the day rotated among the fifteen gentlemen members. Each hit the woods and waters in the hope of bringing back something exceptional to outdo the others. Everyone, as a result, ate like true trenchermen: wildfowl, sturgeon and moose in the fall; beaver, otter, wildcat and raccoon in winter. There was wine, peas, beans, rice, prunes, raisins, dry cod and oil and butter. A specialty for dessert sounds suspiciously like the first crabapple jelly—"certain small fruits like small apples coloured red, of which we made jelly," wrote Lescarbot. And, there were toasts, lots and lots of toasts to go with the singing of folk songs and rounds that pushed the festivities deep into the night. "Whatever our gourmands at home may think," observed Lescarbot, "we found as good cheer at Port-Royal as they in Paris and at a cheaper rate."

Of course it couldn't last. One day in 1608 they arose and noticed a small ship on the horizon. Bad news: de Monts's monopoly had been cancelled. He had done nothing to establish the fur trade; worse, he and a few others may have defrauded the enterprise's backers, which is something that *never* gets mentioned when someone in my family gets bragging. The company was dissolved and the lot of them were to return to France. Champlain and de Monts by then were already more interested in "Canada," the St. Lawrence region where they would found Quebec.

Only Poutrincourt held on to his dream of turning Port Royal into a new world paradise. Back in Paris he presented the French monarch with some Canadian geese, corn, wheat, rye, barley and oats and showed him a knife made out of New World iron. He talked about Membertou's interest in the French monarch and the native curiosity about the Christian faith. Henri bought it. Poutrincourt and his son took some Jesuit priests and returned to the habitation, which Membertou and his folk had been minding in the meantime.

For another four years they scratched out an existence. Meantime, on the strength of Cabot's explorations, England claimed all lands north of Florida. In 1613 an English raiding party travelled the Atlantic seaboard, burning and plundering all the French settlements it could find. They arrived at Port Royal by moonlight with most of the inhabitants on work detail or visiting their Indian friends. With no opposition to stop them the Virginians rounded up pigs, horses and colts and herded them onto the

English ships They took hammer and pick to the huge boulder nearby, obliterating the carved fleurs-de-lys, the triangular hillocks of de Monts's coat of arms and Poutrincourt's family's lion. When the French returned they found nothing but smouldering ruins.

I stand a few feet from where the Virginians sailed in, sucking on cold coffee from a Styrofoam cup while wondering what the whole futile effort meant. For that was pretty much it. Poutrincourt, still desperate for glory, died back in France, his sword drawn, shouting "Kill, kill! God save the King and Poutrincourt," shot by one of his allies during a civil uprising. As for the habitation, Poutrincourt's son kept it up for a while. Then he died. In the great French–English war over the continent that followed, French, English or Indian forces besieged the citadel innumerable times and it changed hands repeatedly. With British conquest in 1710, Port Royal became Annapolis Royal, the lovely little town that now stands nearby. Three years later a treaty gave mainland Nova Scotia to the English; the French kept Cape Breton Island.

This, of course, is history on the grand scale. The sort of thing you can't escape in the school textbooks growing up. Important things had to happen here, midway between the New World and the Old. For everything after flowed from Port Royal. If, for instance, Biencourt had not asserted the French presence here, it is possible that this territory would not have been returned to France by the Treaty of Saint Germain-en-Laye in 1632. Then the best-known event in Nova Scotia's history would never have occurred.

I speak here about the Expulsion of the Acadians, the 1755 deportation of an entire French-speaking people to France, the West Indies and the French possessions along the Mississippi because they refused to take an oath of allegiance to the British Crown. It is more than just a slice of history. The yarn of a Paradise Lost and its martyred people provides a proper context for a place through which a mist of sadness—a wisp of "what if"—habitually drifts. The irony is that the man responsible for the myth, Henry Wadsworth Longfellow, was an American who never came here. But *Evangeline, A Tale of Acadie* was some of the best PR the province ever got.

Acadia, which back then meant an area roughly equivalent to the provinces of New Brunswick and Nova Scotia, was not quite as sumptuous as the ancient Greek Vale of Arcady, that idyllic landscape where nymphs danced and shepherds piped. But the ten thousand French living mainly around the Bay of Fundy had turned it into something startlingly special: instead of clearing and cultivating the uplands they used their experience with the salt marshes of France to build an elaborate system of dykes that allowed excess fresh water to flow back to the Bay while protecting the land from the salt water flooding at high tide. So life by eighteenth-century standards was sweet: no famine, no drought, an adequate-enough diet to keep epidemic away. Longfellow made the place sound like the Garden of Eden and introduced the reader to Évangéline and Gabriel, whose romantic idyll was cruelly interrupted by the English deportation order. The lovers roamed

America searching for each other, only to be reunited when the prematurely old heroine ends her wandering and becomes a Sister of Mercy in Philadelphia, where she finds Gabriel, now dying in a hospital.

The Acadians came back. To me that was the amazing thing. It would be patently stupid to make any parallels between their return and my coming back 250 years later. But at some level we felt the same pull. They arrived in leaky, decrepit boats or on foot from as far away as Massachusetts, walking all the way up through Maine and New Brunswick. This time most of them agreed to take the British oath of allegiance, allowing them to stay. But only in small groups, in designated areas, far from their original lush lands, which had been given away to the English. And never would they forget.

One day in Moncton, N.B., just a few miles' drive from the Nova Scotia border, I went to something called the World Acadian Congress on the campus of the Université de Moncton. I walked around and looked at the historical displays, listened to some Acadian music, both bouncy and mournful, and spent some time in a gymnasium looking at huge family trees taped to the walls. Then I went outside to stand in the sunlight amongst all the thousands of happy, proud people wearing nametags that identified them as Daigles, Theriaults, Arsenaults, Doucets, Savoies, Bastaraches, Chiassons, Maillets, Michauds, Cormiers and LeBlancs. A celebration of survival. At one point I sidled over to a big tent where a tubby guy stirred a pot of gumbo with wide circles of his thick, hairy arm. Petite Cliff LeBlanc was a chef down in Abbeville, La., near where his folk had settled after the diaspora.

"We got them bluish-green eyes that sparkle," he drawled. "That's how I tell who my people are. We all come from the same place, we're all Acadians."

That spirit, more resolute than ever after all this time. I marvel at it as I move along the southwest shore of Nova Scotia, through the township of Clare with Rev. Al Green blasting on the stereo. Off to the right are low trees and some rolling hills, and on the other side, the Atlantic Ocean, blue as the Mediterranean. Somewhere along the road things begin to change. Brilliantly painted homes, far more colourful than the ones owned by English, break the view. Acadian flags—red for courage, white for purity, blue for the sea with a yellow star for the Virgin Mary, patron saint of the Acadians—ripple in the breeze. I pass church after church, big granite things that break the sky with their steeples. The French shore is really one main street, thirty miles long, populated on each side by the descendants of those lively, resilient souls. Cap Ste-Marie becomes St. Alphonse, Meteghan becomes Saulnierville, Comeauville segues into Little Brook, Grosses Coques slides into Beliveaus Cove, and St. Bernard becomes New Edinburgh, despite its name still a French settlement.

Longing to be part of this vibrant, tough culture—literally to taste it—I pull into a roadside takeout spot advertising rappie pie, the local delicacy. Now this is a new one for me, even though I fancy myself a connoisseur of road eats, a person who feels eminently qualified to nominate the club sandwich as Nova Scotia's official dish, it being the one thing you can safely order in the most forlorn eatery in the least-travelled back road and still stay clear of the emergency ward. I can immediately tell that rappie pie, or at least this version of it, does not come with that guarantee. I explore with my plastic fork, testing the semi-gelatinous consistency, take another bite and notice that it has no discernible taste, drive over by the garbage can, roll down the car window and toss the whole thing.

Maybe it travels well and held the Acadians over on their biblical exodus back. Around here few things are only what they seem and just about everything seems to have deeper resonance. It is so hard to avoid traces of history. Nova Scotia is lousy with museums, replicas of famous forts, ships and habitations and plaques to commemorate some long-dead person who did who knows what, God knows when. There's a curiously egalitarian view of the past that treats all events with the same gravity.

Don't take my word for it. Along the South Shore you pass the home of Phil Scott, the world's champion log roller, the signs announcing authentic woollen mills, lighthouses, "the oldest non-conformist church in Canada" and "the home of the Cape Islander lobster fishing boat" amidst the signs for bingo and "access to the Internet." I mean, how is a person to know whether the Archelaus Smith Museum on Cape Sable Island is important or whether time would be better spent having a look at Port La Tour, named after the Huguenot nobleman who founded the place four hundred years ago and fought a decades-long war against a commercial and political rival that cost him his wife and his empire?

There is no way of knowing. Just as there is no way of knowing that the simple sign a couple of clicks south of Shelburne that states "Birchtown, site of the black Loyalist landing in 1783" commemorates something truly special. Birchtown is not a village or a settlement; it is a sign with a few smallish houses and a population of about two dozen, a number of whom are black. That in itself is not unusual; Nova Scotia has a large black population. That so few of the residents of Birchtown are black is what is really odd. Once, when this was the first settlement of free blacks outside Africa, there were black people living there named Robert George Bridges, Boston King, Nathaniel Snowball, Isabel Gibbins, Cesar Perth, Cato Perkins and Moses Wilkinson. Once among their people were ship carpenters, boat builders, caulkers, anchorsmiths, sailmakers, labourers and rope makers; sawyers, millers, shoemakers, coopers, blacksmiths, tanners and skinners; carpenters, painters, gardeners, farmers, fishermen, pilots, sailors, seamen, bakers, tailors and chimney sweeps; a seamstress, a clothier, a milliner, a coachman, a carman and a doctor. They had skills, schools for their children, and their own churches, including one ministered by David George, a Baptist minister who had founded the first black church in America a decade earlier. Most of all they had freedom, or at least a piece of paper saying they were free.

Before that they were servants and slaves in the American South. Then came the Revolutionary War. No definitive record exists of how many served on either side in the conflict. But it is safe to say that more fought with the Loyalists, who promised them land, rations and independence, than stuck with the continental army. They fought valiantly for freedom, then landed in New York during the final days of the Revolution. The British were showing worrisome signs of reneging on their promises and handing the slaves back to the rebels. A commission was set up to sort out the conflicting claims. But Yankee slave owners took matters into their own hands. Wrote an anguished black refugee named Boston King: "We saw our old masters coming from Virginia, North Carolina and other parts, and seizing upon their slaves in the streets of New York, or even dragging them out of their beds." George Washington insisted all the slaves be returned. Guy Carleton, the British governor-in-chief of North America, refused, agreeing only to compile a list of numbers so that compensation could be paid to the former owners. When the ships left New York harbour fully 2,775 of the 3,000 free black Loyalists selected for immigration headed for Nova Scotia and a place named Port Roseway.

Immigration didn't live up to expectations, not by a long shot. Most of the black Loyalists received no land at all. Instead they were left to work the rocky, barren soil near their shanty town or to work as servants to the white Loyalists at the nearby settlement of Shelburne, for wages as low as fifty or sixty dollars a year. "Many of the poor people were compelled to sell their best gowns for five pounds of flour, in order to support life," King recounted in his autobiography. "When they were parted with all their clothes, even to their blankets, several of them fell down dead in the streets through hunger. Some killed and ate their dogs and cats; and poverty and distress prevailed on every side." In Shelburne, the indentured black servants were cheated of their rations, shackled and whipped for being idle or stubborn, and jailed merely for attending a "negro frolick" or dance. Trifling crimes were punished with brutal severity: a woman named Dianna, convicted for two petty larcenies (a theft under twelve pence) was sentenced to 200 lashes at high noon for the first offence and 150 lashes for the other; a man named Light Horse Jack was given 100 lashes at the hands of the common hangman—20 lashes in front of the jail, 20 lashes at the corner of King St., 20 at the corner of St. John's St. and 20 each at the corners of Ann and St. George's Streets; a man named Thomas stole two pieces of pork from a docked ship and was sentenced to two months of jail and hard labour and 12 lashes.

Unable to work the boulder-strewn land, their services no longer in demand by Shelburne's rapidly dwindling white population, the people of Birchtown sank into squalor and despair. The hapless whites in Shelburne claimed that the blacks had devalued their wages with cheap labour and blamed them for their own sorry lot. One summer day in 1784 hundreds of club-carrying whites ran the blacks into Birchtown, pulled down a bunch of their houses, then went home with that feeling of satisfaction that comes from a good day's work. Visiting Birchtown a few years later, an aide to Prince William Henry (later King William IV) wrote back home that the place was "beyond description wretched, situated on the coast in the middle of barren rocks, and partly surrounded by a thick impenetrable wood. Their huts too miserable to guard against the inclemency of a Nova Scotia winter, and their existence almost depending on what they could lay up in summer ... I think I never saw wretchedness and poverty so strongly perceptible in the garb and the countenance of the human species as in these miserable outcasts."

Thomas Peters was fifty-three, an old man by the day's standards. He escaped slavery in North Carolina during the Revolution, joined the British forces, rose to sergeant in a black regiment and sailed as a freeman with the first wave of Loyalist refugees to Nova Scotia. Peters was uneducated, but possessed charisma and enough righteous indignation to speak for all the blacks who escaped from their rebel masters and came to New Brunswick and Nova Scotia expecting Britain to keep its promises. Between 1784 and 1790 Peters petitioned the crown three times for land on behalf of the blacks who settled in New Brunswick. When that got nowhere he organized a fourth petition on behalf of black families in the two provinces and made his way to London, where he planned to present it to the authorities in person.

He landed in London at an ideal moment: liberal guilt over the slave trade was sweeping England; a group of British abolitionists had pooled their resources and obtained a grant of land to establish a free colony of blacks in Sierra Leone. Then Peters arrived with his disturbing accounts of the suffering and disappointment endured by the Loyalist blacks in Nova Scotia. The British Home Office decreed that agents be appointed to provide the dissatisfied black Loyalists with three options: stay in Canada and receive a comfortable settlement for their hardships; join the black army corps in the West Indies or accept free passage to Sierra Leone.

Back in Nova Scotia, Peters and John Clarkson, the main recruiter for the Sierra Leone Company, met self-interested politicians, businessmen who concocted false debts to try to hold on to their cheap labour pool, and free blacks convinced that Sierra Leone was more delusion than opportunity. Ultimately the present was too awful, the future too alluring. By the new year, 600 blacks from Shelburne and Birchtown, 200 from Preston, near Halifax, 180 from the Annapolis Royal–Digby area and 200 from New Brunswick gathered in Halifax. At the insistence of Clarkson, the shipowners gave each captain written instructions to treat the blacks with the respect due all paying customers. One January day in 1792 he was rowed out to each of the fifteen vessels anchored in Halifax harbour to hand the black families assembled on deck signed certificates entitling them to Sierra Leone land. Five days later a favourable wind rose, and the convoy left behind the country that never showed them a moment's decency.

The voyage lasted nearly two months; sixty-five died in the crossing. Clarkson, who lay helpless for a month with a raging fever, almost joined them, then rebounded enough to make landfall. In wilting heat the boats continued up the broad estuary of the Sierra Leone River. They saw the low coastline, the crescendo of hills rising to, in Clarkson's words, "lofty mountains crowned with perpetual verdure." Finally, home. Yet there they met more frustration over land grants. Fearful of reliving the Birchtown experience, they took up arms. But the riot was quelled and the Nova Scotian influence waned in the new colony. Until, that is, 1992, when gunfire again rang through the streets of Freetown, and Valentine Strasser, a Creole descended from the Nova Scotians, became Sierra Leone's president.

Out of curiosity one day I called on Elizabeth Cromwell, who lived in Birchtown, and asked what had happened to the blacks who stayed behind. She told me the last of the elders had died a decade earlier. But since then a few descendants of the settlers had trickled back. Four black families in Birchtown could trace their roots to the great drama. They are the backbone of the local historical society, which pushed the province for the highway sign. They are the ones who cajoled the government into putting up the money for an archaeological survey of the site. It is our history, she explained.

And it is mine too, even though I'm a white boy who grew up in the city. I hold on to the story of Birchtown, the ones who left, the ones who came back, for the same reason I hold on to the story of the Acadians and the other peoples who are patently not me. For in Nova Scotia there is history that exists in the air, floating high above our mundane existence of day-care, sinus headaches and the Goods and Services Tax. Forming us, becoming part of us. It is why we hear despair in the waves pounding the headland. And laughter in the wind.

Three

By the Rattly-Eyed Jesus

—

LET'S ALLOW FOR A SECOND THAT MAYBE THE BIG THINKERS ARE RIGHT. MAYBE myth expresses life far better than history, science or any of the provable things. Doesn't matter at all if they are true, just that they are *your* myths, your fables. I hear "the stories," which seem carried along by the very light and the breeze, and I know they have meaning. They are the subconsciousness of home sure as landscape is the atmosphere, history the collective memory. Deconstruct them and you'll reach some kind of essential truth about Nova Scotia's inner vision. But to do so is the death of fun—like searching for signs of racial alienation in an Oscar Peterson solo. Or seeking to glimpse the scars of an overbearing parent in a Wayne Gretzky end-to-end rush.

Some of the myths seem to have no real origin. It's as though they existed before everything else. In the beginning, say the Mi'kmaqs, was Glooscap, their giant warrior hero whom the Great Spirit endowed with supernatural powers. At the dawn of civilization he lay on his back, head to the rising Sun, feet to the setting of the Sun, left hand to the south, right hand the north. After seventy times seven nights and days a bent old woman born that very day came to him—the grandmother who owed her existence to the dew on the rock. The next day at noon a young man came to Glooscap. He owed his existence to the beautiful foam on the waters, and Glooscap called him My Sister's Son. The following noon another person appeared—the mother of all Mi'kmaqs.

Before leaving for the Happy Hunting Grounds, Glooscap taught his people how to make canoes and he cleared rivers and streams for navigation. Once he was taking a bath in a trench dug out for him by Beaver. His friend Whale swam in and refused to leave until Glooscap walked to shore. Glooscap got up, and Whale swam away with such force that the great tides of the Bay of Fundy slosh back and forth to this day. Once Glooscap changed into a beaver, grew angry and slapped his tail on the waters of the Bay of Fundy five times with such force that five islands were created. Another time Beaver's dam caused the waters to overflow into Glooscap's garden. In anger, he hurled a stone but missed, instead cutting Digby Neck into the Bay of Fundy.

These are the timeless stories that concretize the spiritual, creative essentials of our world. But along with the real myths of the natives a new land like Nova Scotia is infused with the old-world mythology and folk beliefs that came with the settlers. The very name, Acadia, with the hopes and expectations that go along with it, harkens back to those origins. So does an abiding belief in fore-runners, ghost ships, monsters lurking in lakes and woods and cloven-foot devils, tales that can be traced to the harbours of England, the dales of Scotland and the villages of Germany. Stories like these help the explainable harden into pure fact.

Yet there are also stories that linger because they remain forever mysteries. The *Mary Celeste* was a wonder of workmanship, one in a long line of hardy vessels that rolled into the ocean at Spencer's Island, another tiny Nova Scotia community that produced fantastic sailing ships during the last half of the nineteenth century. Christened the *Amazon* when she was launched in 1861, the brigantine changed her name seven years later after a freak accident in a gale. Some Americans salvaged her, and on the morning of November 7, 1872, *Mary Celeste* left New York for Genoa, loaded with a cargo of coal, hay and liquor. Onboard was master mariner Benjamin Spooner Briggs, his wife, Sara, two-year-old daughter Sophia, and a small crew of seven.

On December 4 another brigantine, the *Dei Grata,* also Nova Scotia–built, was making her way to Gibraltar from New York. It had been a stormy crossing for the most part, and halfway between the Azores and Portugal the captain of the *Dei Grata* spotted sails on the horizon. It was the *Mary Celeste.* The seas were high but not dangerous. Three of the *Dei Grata*'s crewmen made it onboard. It was deserted. Two of the sails had blown away. Some of the rigging was gone. One of the lifeboats was missing but there was no sign that the tackle had been used to put it over the side. There was water in the hold, the binnacle was knocked over, the compass in the cabin smashed and the kitchen stove had been knocked out of place. Otherwise everything seemed orderly: gear stowed properly; plenty of still-warm food and water; the child's toys and clothes scattered around an unmade bed. The captain's sword was still under his bed. But his sextant, chronometer, navigation books and ship's papers were missing. The final entry in the ship's log read, "Monday, November 25. At 8 Eastern Point bore S.S.W. 6 miles distant."

It had sailed on for 378 miles with no one at the helm and no one aboard. Back ashore at least four men surfaced claiming to be survivors of the *Mary Celeste,* but knew none of the details of the voyage or the ship. Newspaper stories periodically speculated that it was all an elaborate murder plot; books postulated the whole thing was some kind of insurance scam. But no answers, just theories. So the story lives on, adding another layer to life here.

Just knowing about it colours your view of the world, particularly when you sit eating your lunch on a log on the beach at Spencer's Island, looking at the pillars of an old wharf where the *Mary Celeste* was once tied. I get the same odd feeling whenever I look west across Mahone Bay, which is usually how I view the province's best-known island. To reach it you have to head down Route 324 and drive through Gold River and Western Shore until you see a sign for the Oak Island Inn ("Cable television, tennis courts, murder-mystery weekends"). Cross the causeway, pass a few anchored fishing skiffs and the kids splashing in the water, drive through a wooden gate with a misspelled sign bearing a skull and crossbones and stop in the clearing. Last time I was there two military tents snapped in the wind along the waterline. Twenty yards away a couple of men struggled to raise a giant inflatable Keith's Beer can.

I was excited. The first time anybody really got animated about Oak Island was in the summer of 1795, when a boy named Daniel McGinnis rowed out to it and walked about a mile through the woods to the eastern end. On the top of a small hill he found a tackle block hanging from the branches of an oak. Below the tree was a slight depression in the earth that looked as if it had been worked on some years earlier. In the late eighteenth century this part of the coast was well known as a pirate haunt. There was a persistent story of an old man who on his New England deathbed confessed to having been one of Captain Kidd's crew and to helping bury "over two millions of money" beneath the soil of a secluded island east of Boston. So young Daniel raced home, got a couple of friends and some shovels and rowed back. Two feet down, the boys hit a layer of flagstones and under it found a 13-foot-wide shaft. Ten feet down, they found a layer of logs tightly pressed together. Ten feet deeper another log platform, and ten feet below it, another.

At this point, exhausted, they marked the spot, covered the pit with trees and brush and quit, determined to return. They never did, unable to find anyone willing or able to help with the dig. The story lived on, though. A few years later some local businessmen dug down through the pit and discovered charcoal and coconut fibre and more log platforms at ten-foot intervals. Beyond ninety feet they found a stone inscribed with hieroglyphics that, according to one translation, said, "Forty feet below, two million pounds are buried." At 98 feet, they hit something hard, perhaps a treasure chest. They came back in the morning to find the shaft full of sea water. When they tried to bail it out, the water kept coming in. Whoever had dug the shaft had also dug at least two tunnels that filled the pit with water when the inscribed capstone was removed.

The treasure hunters packed it in. Other groups took a whack at it, their drills bringing up links from a gold watch and tiny pieces of parchment—each new tantalizing hint touching off more speculation about the treasure's origins. I particularly like the latest one: that it all has to do with the travels of Prince Henry Sinclair of the Orkney Islands back in the final days of the fourteenth century. Legend has it that after hearing about a strange but magnificent land teeming with fish and cannibals, he and a crew set sail for Newfoundland and what became the Maritime provinces. Sinclair was a supporter of the Knights Templar movement in Europe, to the point where he provided refuge in the Orkneys for Templars being persecuted on the continent by the ruling princes of Europe jealous of their wealth (the Templars were supposed to have become the custodians of the Holy Grail). There are those who think that Sinclair and his Templar friends may have buried the Grail in Nova Scotia—on Oak Island—which they intended to use as some kind of new refuge, a new Jerusalem. But there are also those who think that buried at the bottom of that impenetrable pit lies Marie Antoinette's jewels, the secret stash of Sir Francis Drake, the long-lost manuscripts of Francis Bacon, the booty of Blackbeard or Morgan the Pirate.

Most Nova Scotians, on the other hand, still cling to the old theory that Capt. William Kidd buried his treasure there before the British hanged him in 1701.

"That's bullshit," barks Dan Blakenship, striding angrily from the small museum at the back of the lot. "All of Kidd's whereabouts were known. It's a theory that doesn't stand up to scrutiny." Ruddy-faced, with wide shoulders and a big blackened blister on one of his cigar-like fingers, Blakenship is seventy-two but looks a decade younger. He knows a thing or two about theories. Thirty years before, he chucked a successful career as a general contractor in Florida after reading a *Reader's Digest* article about the Oak Island hunt. If he harboured any doubts about his career change, they disappeared in 1971, when a television probe lowered down the shaft sent back pictures of what looked like a chest and tools. Watching the monitor of the closed-circuit camera, Blakenship believes he saw a severed human head float across the screen, as well as a preserved human body slumped on the chest. So he was already a believer when he became field manager for Triton Alliance, a consortium of Canadian and American investors fascinated with the Oak Island legend.

Today he is in a foul mood as he stands with some young underlings in a clearing near the entrance to the mine shaft. Two days from now everything has to be just so for the hundreds of visitors expected for the special bicentennial celebration of the Big Dig. The highlight of the event: the unveiling of a five-foot-high concrete stone to honour the six men who have died so far in the hunt. But what really bothers him is the feeling that the whole thing—the twenty years and $140,000 of his own money spent pursuing his obsession—might be for nothing. We pile into a half-ton and make the short, bumpy drive back to the compound. Outside again, Blakenship squints into the sun, plants his feet, folds his arms and tells me the tale of his betrayal. How Triton, in which Blakenship is a minority shareholder, had refused his request for the $350,000 more he says he needs to solve the mystery. How instead they inked a deal with Oak Island Discoveries, owned by a Boston millionaire and an Emmy-winning film director, which wanted to conduct its extensive scientific research of the site.

"My partners seem to have a new theory every six months," says Blakenship, who is on the move again, heading towards the tents erected to house the celebrations. "I'd rather tell you who it *could* have been. Whoever did it took many years to complete the job. We only know 10 per cent of what went on there. You have to look for someone with the time, the purpose and the drive. Who controlled religion at the time? The Knights Templar. They controlled all the wealth in Europe and the Mediterranean. They controlled all the shipping. They were looking for a new world. As far as possible you have to look at the evidence. Nolan"—a competing treasure hunter—"found a perfect symmetrical cross at the end of the island. I think there is something to it. I'm not saying it was the Knights Templar. But there's a good possibility. I will say it has merit."

The most merit of any of the theories? I ask.

"Well, that's a strong statement," he says, and pauses. I can hear the surf break, the wind jostling the tall oaks, just as it always has on the island. "I'll just say it has merit."

Stories like Oak Island live on because they are haunting and wonderful. But in Nova Scotia even the apocryphal-sounding yarns—the tall tales—have a faint ring of truth. What is one to make of the story about the Cape Breton mortician who opened his door one day and found a couple of boys off the fishing boats with a body they'd hauled from the ocean? None of them recognized the unfortunate's face. So the undertaker reached the novel conclusion of pumping the cadaver full of embalming fluid, clothing it in a nice suit and propping the body up in the corner in the hope of jogging someone's memory. Nobody recognized the body though, and after eleven months he gave up and buried the corpse. It was forgotten about until he received a call from a mortician in the United States who explained that the body was likely that of a sailor from Maine who had gone missing at sea. The remains were dug up and the casket stuck on a train, bound for a proper funeral. As an afterthought, and a rare moment of professional vanity, the undertaker from Cape Breton pinned to the body a note for his counterpart handling the wake at the other end. It read: "You can open it if you want."

Now, true or not, I love that tale, which seems as perfectly formed, as funny, horrible and true as a Flannery O'Connor short story. Some, admittedly, are less original. Take this variation on the old ashes-as-egg-timer joke, which involves a woman I know from Lunenburg County, a widow whose husband died early leaving her to raise three kids alone. When they were all grown and gone and she was well into middle age, she remarried, a doctor who had immigrated from Scotland and was renowned for his frugality. He died too. One day a visitor arrived to make sure she was coping with widowhood. (It helps here to imagine the local dialect, the extreme lilt and emphasis on unusual words and syllables that stretches and transforms the county's name, for instance, into *Loon-an-bahg,* which always sounds to me like an accounting firm in a Monty Python routine.)

"Well you know the docta he left all his money to charity you know," she said, cocking an eyebrow. "But you know he was a funny one. All he left me was that old Volkswagen of his. I was very angry about the whole thing. Very angry."

I can imagine, said the visitor.

"Now you know things are funny. All along he told me that he wanted his ashes sprinkled on this loch back tha in Scotland. So his day did come."

She walks her guest towards the mantelpiece where an urn stands. Pauses, then gives a conspiratorial wink and says, "Thaas the bastard—I've got him now."

It is no wonder we are the way we are. By the standards of the land my family's stories are nothing exceptional, not by a long shot. But my personal mythology includes mine cave-ins, race riots, the carnage of Vimy Ridge and strike breakers riding down innocent people in the streets. It includes murderers and heroes, wondrous athletes and monumental drunks, geniuses and idiots, the pious and the profane.

Then there are the words. They matter, for they are the way we deliver the myths and stories of our world into day-to-day life. Language marks Nova Scotia, a modern-day Tower of Babel where a traveller will hear Gaelic, French, English and German within a couple of hours. When all those dissonant sounds mix together the result can be truly startling—weird words that carry a world of meaning in the slightest inflection and volumes of social history in a single phrase.

Lewis Poteet, an English professor from Montreal who summered on the South Shore, was so fascinated with the jumble of words and phrases there that he began to collect and study them. Eventually he published a South Shore phrase book, which makes a great read. If, for instance, you drive around Mahone Bay you may hear someone called a *semiquibber* (idiot) or *flutterbug* (easily excitable). You may hear someone refer to *gurry* (waste from cleaning fish) or a *lambkiller* (a severe, sudden March storm). You may hear somebody talk about *moger* (wretched), *forelaying* (expecting), being *swonked* (exhausted) or *iglish* (grouchy). When people from the *real* South Shore get wound up they might blurt *holy snappin' assholes, gookemole, holy old twist, kroppy doppy, hold your pickle* or *by the rattly-eyed Jesus*. An older man might call a younger one *old son* and a young, green hired hand might be called *nubbins*. If they think a fuss is being made over something unimportant they might call it *a fart in a windstorm*. If they doubt what you are saying their response might be *I'll tow that one alongside for a bit before I bring it aboard.* An unattractive person might be called *homely as a stump fence,* a drunk is all *snapped up,* someone with a big butt is *three axehandles across the ass.* And the warning *Don't stick out your bruddle at me, you'll be mootsen someplace else* means you're in deep shit.

Words still matter around here. This is a society where the keepers of the stories—the tribal elders—are still revered. One morning, I made an appointment to see Joe Casey, the MLA from Digby, a prosperous fishing village in the Bay of Fundy, who seems happy to talk to a visitor even if he has no idea what I wanted. His office is in a hideous little strip mall on the way into town. Casey, who is seventy-seven, turns out to be a jolly, gentlemanly Bay of Fundy Mark Twain. He wears a navy blazer and one of those Zorba the Greek fishing captain's hats and sits at a desk amidst the memorabilia from his varied career, the stories rolling off his lips like pearls. Quite a résumé: six times elected to the Nova Scotia legislature, World War Two naval officer, fisherman, fishplant operator, steamship pilot, raconteur. No great statesman, as a politician his contribution could be best summed up by a bill he tabled:

MISTER JOSEPH CASEY: Mr. Speaker, I hereby give notice that on a future day I shall move the adoption of the following resolution:

Whereas Frankland Theriault of Weymouth has been ordered by the Egg Marketing Board to keep no more than 499 hens; and

Whereas the stores in Digby area have been threatened with prosecution if they continue to sell his product; and

Whereas Mr. Theriault is semi-retired due to a heart condition; and

Whereas he is asking only that he be allowed to continue for two years in the business, to allow him to build up a nest-egg before receiving his old age pension;

Be it resolved that the provincial government not be allowed to enforce mandatory birth control, euthanasia or genocide in the hen house; and

Be it resolved, to paraphrase the Prime Minister of Canada, the State has no business in the hen houses of the nation.

He can talk: one minute he's talking about such locals as Zippy Moses, Ernie Balser, an old couple named Torchy and Drindy and places named Bummer's Crossing. Then without a pause he's moved on to Jimmy Cagney and Arthur Kennedy, who used to vacation in the area, his long speech before the Indian parliament, manoeuvring oil tankers through dangerous waters and impenetrable fog and pulling drowned friends out of the Bay.

"One night the telephone rang by my bed," he told me. "I picked it up and a man asked, 'Can I walk an elephant up Digby wharf?' Thinking he was playing a trick I replied, 'You have a wrong number. You had better call Noah,' and then hung up.

"A few minutes later the phone rang again and the caller asked if I were the harbour pilot or not. When I replied that I was, he said that he needed to bring a circus to Digby by ship and legitimately needed the information about the elephant. The ship on her way to Digby had docked in Yarmouth. While off-loading the animals, the ship had caught on fire. The Yarmouth fire department sprayed so much water into the ship that she rolled over. There were elephants, tigers, monkeys and other circus animals all over town. One of the elephants managed to wander well into the countryside.

"Early next morning an elderly lady looked out of her pantry window and saw an elephant in her garden. She immediately called the RCMP and said, 'Officer, there is the strangest animal in my garden that I have ever seen and you will never believe what he is doing. He is reaching down with his tail and tearing up my cabbages by the roots and guess what he's doing with them!' "

He has so many tales you want to hear them all and remember them all. This province buzzes with voices that, once heard, linger. Ron Caplan could not let them go. He was a gangly, long-haired book designer deeply unhappy with his life in Pittsburgh when he arrived in Cape Breton in 1970. The local culture fascinated him— the Celts, the Acadians, the Mi'kmaqs, the Jamaicans who arrived to work the Sydney coke ovens, the Italian miners. He took a run at a magazine of oral culture and history, published from his home in Wreck Cove, population sixty. According to the first issue, Caplan's baby would be "devoted to the history, natural history and future of Cape Breton Island."

One day I scanned a bunch of back copies at a library in Halifax. Here's Willy Petrie, the diviner, talking about what happens when he's gripping a forked stick and it nears water: "I can't hold it. I can brace my two feet, I can't hold it at all. It'll twist, keep on twisting, I can't stop it. Keep on turning on the end. You just put the prongs across your hands this way. And if it's gonna go it'll go down, you can't hold it. It don't have to move my hand, and it'll twist turn right in my hand. If I've got one anyways big or something, jeez, if I tried to hold it it'd tear me to pieces, the strain on me, the terrible strain on me in trying to hold it."

I liked Marguerite Gallant, ninety, of Chéticamp reminiscing about being thirteen days on the hospital critical list when someone named Leo came to visit and her saying to him: "After I'm dead I will follow you to the Point. And you will see my soul on pebbles, on grains of sand, on little pieces of straw—any place you look. I will be in front of you in fifty different shapes."

I was particularly taken with Bob Fitzgerald, who ran the telephone exchange in Dingwall, considering some of those who lie buried in the soil of Cape Breton: "They were tremendous people. We don't have anything like them. And God bless your soul, I have nothing but respect for them, yes—the most profound respect for them. Every one of them. There's no more left like them and no more to come like them. All you need do sometimes, if you have a little imagination, is roam through the countryside and let your imagination run wild. And you'll travel some of the old farms in this country and you'll stop and look at some of the great rock piles here and there—and how many, when they look at them, how many stop and think of all the sweat and toil and tears it took to put that rock pile there? How many think of it? Very, very few. But if you drive along by one of those old farms some time, and you see one of those old rock piles, just get out and walk over to it and see the thoughts that will go through your mind—and picture the old slaves that dragged those rocks and stones from all around, the land that's cleared, and piled them there. We don't have no more people to work like that today. Somebody'll say we got wise. No, we got foolish. They were the wise people. They had to be."

PART TWO

My Kind of People

I grew up a bluenose,
as Nova Scotians are known,
supposedly after the colour of
potatoes grown there.

Robert MacNeil

——

Four

These Are My People

—

IT WAS FALL WHEN I MOVED BACK TO NOVA SCOTIA. DAYLIGHT SAVINGS TIME, and the long evenings were over. When sundown came you felt the first shudder of winter out there somewhere on the horizon. I was joyfully overwrought, a newly released prisoner running down the street without even feeling the pavement under my feet. Every building, patch of grass, shadow flickered with meaning. Memories snapped by like pictures on a deck of cards. Strangers met my exultant eyes, seemed to smile then look away. These are my people! my heart cried.

I knew I was being foolish. I knew that since I recognized no one, no one must recognize me. But I simply could not rein myself in. My spirit soared as I stumbled down the sidewalk. Any minute a couple of white-jacketed attendants were going to slap a straight-jacket on me and drive siren screaming to the mental hospital across the harbour. I didn't care. It was fall, my favourite time. I felt eighteen again, like I had just emerged from the shower on a Friday night after a basketball game and my friends were waiting at the Midtown Tavern.

There is no such thing as an identity crisis in Nova Scotia; that is maybe the hardest thing for newcomers to understand. While the rest of the country may whinge about the nature of being Canadian, we know who we are, bad as that might be. Not only that, we celebrate ourselves; we revel in our distinctiveness even as the gulf of difference between us and the rest of the country, the continent, the world narrows. The demographic tidal bore into the province may bring cash, jobs and strange new people, but this place holds on to its essence. Its identity. Its character. Even people who live here tend to forget how different we really are. I certainly did, wistful as my memories of Nova Scotia were while I was one of the temporary displaced living away. Very least, I should have remembered our wedding night, a week before we left for Alberta, bound down the eastern shore to an inn called Camelot in a cab owned by a company that probably made as much bootlegging rum as getting people from A to B. Our pilot: a wiry little guy with a Junior B league haircut who begged us to stop for a suspicious-looking delivery inside the Halifax city limits. He tore ass once we hit the highway. Somewhere beside the moonlit ocean he asked would we mind stopping while he said hello to an old girlfriend. A bit much to ask a couple on their honeymoon, but we laughed and said what the hell.

"Jaysus, that's great. Only be a sec," he said breathlessly, slamming the door behind him. "Last time I saw her it didn't end so good. But here goes."

We sat down, our legs dangling off the end of the wharf. An idyllic scene with the boats bobbing and the ropes creaking with the strain. Then, the slam of a screen door and a dog barking. We turned our heads and saw the great lover himself puffing down the trail being pursued by the longest, foulest string of curses I've ever heard lashed together in a single sentence.

We never did find out what happened in there. But I like what the whole scene said. I like that kind of brazen, foolhardy optimism, that willingness to trust in pure wit to keep your head above water, even when there's not a hope in hell you can pull it off. Hard places like Nova Scotia bring out that side of people. To live here you need a sense of lasting tradition, loyalty and common purpose to go with a reckless imagination and rebellious spirit. You also need a healthy dose of self-reliance and a mile-wide streak of pride, the hallmarks of the true survivor. I have a friend who was president of a consulting business in Toronto until he bought a chunk of gorgeous Nova Scotia oceanfront in a place called Musquodoboit to build his dream house. A few months after he moved in he saw a half-ton pull into the next-door driveway. Since the owners were away Ross walked over to investigate. My friend is well over two hundred pounds, has a face like Sean Connery and the bearing of someone who holds a third-degree black belt in karate, which he does. He politely asked the man in the oilskins walking up from the beach if he knew the owners. "I'm a lobster fisherman," was the reply. "We go where we fucking well want."

My friend was puzzled by the encounter. But I take the fisherman's point: life can be hard in Nova Scotia. Who can endure if defeat or demoralization creep in? Nova Scotians fully realize that luck is for other people and that they have to make their own breaks. Sometimes they even do. Otherwise they shake their fists at the gods and at the rest of the world. They yell and curse, brood, dance, fornicate and fight. Because what else is life for?

Nova Scotia is a place where the full scope of humanity seems to fit onto one small stage. And if there is such a thing as the Nova Scotian identity, its soul lies in the sum total of values that exist distinctly in its multitude of people and places. Cape Bretoners, my people, might as well be from another planet as the mainland. Yet even within that small island there's a mind-boggling diversity, the gentle-spirited folk on the gorgeous west coast being as different from the hard-bitten stoics of the industrialized southeast as is humanly possible. Back on the mainland, one minute you're listening to an Acadian shopkeeper ramble on animatedly in French, few miles down the road it's the skirl of the bagpipes and an unblinking stare from some craggy Hebredian face. Hour later you're in some old Loyalist homestead staring at one of those wall hangings embroidered with *There'll always be an England/England shall be free/If England means as much to you/as England means to me*. Or you're down on the moody eastern shore, one of the more depressed spots in the province, with its undercurrent of violence that manifests in anything from race riots to random shootings. Then, before your head has a chance to stop spinning, you're in Lunenburg County, still populated by the descendants of the original Protestant farmers from France, Switzerland and southwestern Germany.

There's room for everyone. Reminds me of what Mark Twain

said at the beginning of *Huckleberry Finn:* "In a barrel of odds and ends it is different; things get mixed up, and the juice kind of swaps around, and the things go better." We are all different and we are all connected. I didn't always understand that. But now as I plunged back into my old life I finally did. Identity is landscape, history and mythology. It is roots and genes. It is a lot of different things, like a Cajun gumbo. The recipe is essentially the same; what changes are a few of the ingredients, the proportions, the spices. It may taste a little different every time, but it's still unmistakably gumbo. It could be nothing else.

Universal truths are, of course, hard to come by. Nevertheless, there are things you should know right from the start about Nova Scotians. Not all of them, of course. The newcomers are adding new flavours to the mix, changing it as the province changes them. But I cannot speak for those people. For now I want to talk about the ones who have been here longer. *My people,* about whom a few broad statements are possible.

Despite the inordinately large number of scholars, scientists and big thinkers risen from their midst, Nova Scotians retain a loud contempt for anything that smells intellectual. Because of circumstances, they tend to defer to authority by bowing and scraping to politicians in Ottawa, to the rich, the church, the big corporations headquartered elsewhere. A habit that has gotten them nowhere and is broken only, it seems, by intemperate action, whether long, unwinnable labour strikes or massive protest votes that only alienate the government in Ottawa.

They look at the world through flinty eyes. Which is fortunate, perhaps, since it prevents them from falling too often prey to shysters, con artists, religious saviours, economic miracle workers and other cheats who gravitate to desperate places. (They leave that to the bureaucrats, so willing to shovel taxpayers' money at sad, doomed heavy water plants that make no heavy water, gold mines that find no gold, oil fields that yield not one barrel of crude.)

They have a penchant for intrigue and scheming—which explains why they rule the world of business, the media, the armed forces and the church once unchained from this small pond. No wonder partisan politics is such a sport, religion and pastime, and Nova Scotians make the wiliest politicians in the land. The world is just different down here, a place where until recently a payoff to the governing party ensured not only that you would get a liquor licence to open a bar but also that any competitor who wanted to open a watering hole nearby would not. There are brand-new roads that go nowhere and gleaming wharfs in villages where no one fishes. If a visitor from some far-away place asks about the incongruity of such a thing the answer usually comes back, "That's just Nova Scotia politics," and somehow they understand.

They are violent and clannish, which makes for good soldiers but bad enemies. Nova Scotians have always been a rowdy, rough lot, a band of hockey-rink brawlers, after-the-dance scrappers, sucker punchers, rock throwers. It is no exaggeration to say that more great boxers have come out of industrial Cape Breton and the North End of Halifax than the rest of the country combined. It is also no exaggeration to say that while there is probably more life on a Saturday night within a square block of New Waterford than in ten miles of Toronto there are probably more dislocated knuckles and flattened septums too. They make them tough here. As an example I offer up a guy I used to see at the Y who owed some money to some bikers from Montreal. They took him to the Angus L. MacDonald bridge, held him over the side and threatened to drop him off unless he paid up. Normally this ploy worked. But our man said something to the effect of "drop away." The bikers looked at each other in puzzlement, stood him up. Then shot him in the knee.

That is not an untypical story. Nova Scotians are no more crime-prone per capita than other Canadians, making them in a global sense next to saints. But who can match the strange, lurid nature, the pulp fiction quality to stories glimpsed on the local evening news and heard in everyday conversation? Opening up a newspaper around here is like cracking a Jim Thompson novel: page one might include a story about the former premier charged with a raft of sexual assaults. The court briefs on page 5 might include the details of a case involving a former crown prosecutor—who was engaged to a woman, even while he was married to someone else who lived a few blocks away from his fiancée in the same subdivision—now being charged with embezzlement. Buried on the same page might be the latest on the war in Moser River: a poisonous little town on the eastern shore where a gang of white trash had been terrorizing the local folk. On another page might be a short story noting that a man had been found guilty of an elaborate hoax to fake his own death by pretending he had been hauled into the ocean by a wave from the much-photographed and visited rocks of Peggy's Cove. I kid you not.

They like their faith in big doses, their heroes doomed and larger than life. They play card games called Tarabish, drink gallons of boiled tea, smoke cartons of cigarettes and down any sort of alcohol they can raise to their lips. Not much has really changed in that regard. "There are 1,000 houses in the town," a Halifax settler wrote home to Britain in the 1750s. "We have upwards of 100 licensed [drinking] houses and perhaps as many without licence, so the business of one half the town is to sell rum and the other half to drink it."

Nova Scotians think the kitchen is the only place for a party. They call everyone Buddy, label anybody who doesn't tuck a napkin into their shirt "big feelin'," call anything that they liked "some good" and anywhere that is not Nova Scotia "away." They have a dark sense of humour, stemming from the fact that catastrophes are what is funny, and if Nova Scotians see more humour than other people, it is perhaps because more things go wrong here than anywhere else.

They tend to treat money with little respect—the quintessential example being the legendary Halifax rummy who spent most of the million he won in the lottery during a vicious month-long drinking binge before giving the rest to his buddies and charity. Conversely they can be cheap, even the rich ones—of which there are a surprising number. Partly that's just an almost pathological desire not to appear showy. Which is why a visitor would have no sense that behind the facade of those big understated houses in old South End Halifax are interiors that drip shipping and brewing wealth, that the great houses looming on the hill in Yarmouth are still furnished with treasures brought back from the Orient during the days of the windjammers, that in bank accounts in small towns throughout the province low-key fortunes still moulder. Roy Jodrey, the sharpy from the Annapolis Valley, may have made millions investing in apples and pulp and paper. But he liked to fly economy to stay one of the boys. Once some friends got him a ticket in business class so he could sit with them. "He planted his fatness in his roomy seat," his biographer Harry Bruce wrote, "glowered at the cabin's luxury, squirmed guiltily and grumbled to no one, 'The people of Hantsport will know about this before I even get home.' "

When it comes to sex they are a surreptitious, darkly randy lot. I have a friend who in his early twenties was carrying on an affair with an acquaintance's aunt. Once, in the middle of the night he climbed an elm tree in the hope of getting into the second-floor bedroom of the house she shared with her nephew and his family. Now my friend once separated his shoulder playing hockey and periodically it pops out of place, sometimes at the worst moments—like when he is thirty feet up a tree at 3 a.m. It's damn painful too. Which, I suppose, was a good thing in this case, because a neighbour heard his agonized moans and called the fire department, who dispatched a hook-and-ladder truck. They detreed my friend as his lover and her family watched from the window in sleepy-eyed disbelief.

Thus it has always been. Why else would the name Ada mean so much to generations of Halifax males? True, Ada McCallum may have been no Doll Tearsheet, the madam who operated in Halifax during the early 1940s, wore a fur coat and smart dresses, patronized the best shops and restaurants and set her girls up in snug flats and apartments or in secluded cottages well outside the city. She might not even have had quite the clout of Doll's successor, Germaine, the Paris-born boss at 51 Hollis St., which was directly across from the back door of Government House, the Lieutenant Governor's residence. (According to legend, a respectable South End burgher once died in the arms of one of her girls. Germaine made a couple of discreet phone calls and some of his friends showed up and carted the body to the steps of the respected Halifax Club. The press dutifully reported that he'd collapsed and died entering his beloved haunt.) Even so, Ada, who once had as a boyfriend an editorial executive at the newspaper where I worked, lived out her final years in the company of an eccentric gentleman of leisure from Iceland who claimed to be a graduate of the London School of Economics and a one-time concert pianist. When she died in 1986 at the age of seventy-eight—leaving the operation to some of her kids—the newspapers celebrated her career, remembering her as a "beautiful, socially accomplished woman" who, after becoming a madam, still hobnobbed with unsuspecting admirals, generals and South End snobs.

These are my people. They all are. Because we are all connected in bigger or smaller ways. A frightening thought sometimes, in a tavern or mall somewhere or staring down from the visitors' gallery at the provincial legislature during Question Period. But what do they see when I pass by, still giddy about having moved back home? A man wearing a goofy expectant look. Nodding at people he has never met before. As if to long-lost friends.

Five

Are Ye One of the Biscuit-Foot MacKinnons?

—

I DO NOT HAVE A GOOD SENSE OF DIRECTION. LET ME START AGAIN: I HAVE A poor sense of direction. Okay, let's be frank—I get lost a lot. So often that it is never a surprise, so often that I have taken to building into itineraries a certain amount of time spent travelling in the wrong direction. Even in the most familiar places I routinely let my mind wander and forget where I'm going. Exciting, in a way: when I jump into a car I really could end up anywhere. Left, right, it's all the same to me because it's as though I'm seeing everything for the very first time. Sometimes I magically arrive where I'm supposed to be going, blissfully unaware of how I got there. That's as close as I get to being certain of the existence of a higher power.

No matter how many times I've been there, I always fail to take the right turn to Antigonish, which given the dearth of other possible exits is a singularly bad piece of driving. The result: I hit town an hour after the 10,000-metre foot race, just as the pipe band championships are getting under way down at the Antigonish Highland Games at Columbus Field. I pull into the parking lot at Piper's Pub, the town's liveliest watering hole, where John Pellerin, the amiable bartender/fiddler, helps me find the last motel room in town. A lovely, carefree day. Outside everyone is taking their time walking under the sun, which has finally slipped through the clouds.

I am here because Antigonish, as the local promotional literature likes to say, "is the centre of the province's Highland Heart." A nice phrase, and it even has the virtue of being true. While I'm talking to Pellerin someone named Donald MacDonald walks up. It is a name you run across in these parts. Just out of curiosity I pick up the phone book on the bar and open it under Antigonish (the town being too small to warrant its own directory). There I find seventeen Donald MacDonalds, one Donnie MacDonald and two Donna MacDonalds. I also run my thumb down an even dozen John Chisholms and eleven John Macleans. No wonder people in Antigonish County, neighbouring Pictou County and Scottish-flavoured Cape Breton Island are so dependent on nicknames to keep everyone straight. In the run of a couple of hours I've already run across Andrew "G'day" MacDonald, "Lucky" John C. MacDonald, Billy Collie Billy MacDonald, who is most definitely not to be confused with Collie Hughie MacDonald, and Ronnie "D.D." MacDonald, whose immediate family is known as "The D.D.s".

The layers of names often conjure up the ghosts of ancestors. John Angus Andrew Hughie MacIsaac—I create this name at random, although I have no doubt that such a person exists somewhere in Nova Scotia—could have had a father named Angus, a great-grandfather named Andrew and a great-great-grandfather named Hughie. Sometimes, the nicknames refer to a physical feature, an occupation or where a family lives. Other times, they refer to some piece of family history. I remember a conversation with Richard MacKinnon, who teaches at the University College of Cape Breton, in Sydney, and is an expert on Celtic nicknames. To prove a point he told me about a great-uncle living in Glace Bay who tried to steal a barrel of biscuits from the mine company store during the bloody labour riots of the 1930s and ended up breaking a toe when he dropped the barrel on his foot. MacKinnon had pretty much forgotten about the whole sorry episode until he gave a lecture on Highland names at the University of New Brunswick, in Fredericton. Once finished he asked for questions. A shaky hand went up in the back of the room. "Excuse me, Mr. MacKinnon," said an ancient, quavery voice, "but are ye one of the Biscuit-Foot MacKinnons?"

Of course, I am not the first person to discover that Nova Scotians are more or less a tribe. If, say, a person named MacIsaac came down from Toronto to a wedding they wouldn't make it to the bar and back before somebody would be wondering aloud whether they were related to the MacIsaacs of Judique. Someone would know Merle from his newspapering days. Someone else went to father Dunc MacIsaac's parish. Someone would have kids who were taught by Al. Someone else would have gone to St. Francis Xavier University in Antigonish (everyone here just calls it St. F. X.) with one of the other seven kids in the immediate family. And so the conversation would go floating on like a jazz solo until someone finally changed the subject. Tribe, you see, matters here. It is at the root of the great events and the small dramas. I recall a stag party thrown for a guy marrying a woman from a family I knew. It began convivially enough but ended with the father of the bride and his half-dozen sons and brothers standing back to back swinging it out with the groom and his father, brothers and uncles. A couple of days later they were casting dark glances from opposite sides of the church as the couple said their wedding vows. And now they are family, even if just by marriage—which means that while the bad blood may forever linger between the two clans, God help anyone from outside dim enough to take a swing at a member of either house at some distant stag.

Blind, unquestioning loyalty definitely has a downside—"I was just doing my duty" being the last words every war criminal utters before the hangman opens the trapdoor. But it is good to know that no matter how bad it gets, there are always those who will have you. Home, as someone somewhere once said, is the one place where you can go and not be turned away. I say amen to that. It warms my heart to know that if I were on the run with the bloodhounds coming a mile back, there is always my tribe, with its boundaries and rivalries that extend beyond simple blood ties. This tribal sense of loyalty cuts many different ways. Protestants versus Catholics, Pictou versus New Glasgow, islanders versus mainlanders. You see it in fist fights after hockey games and in the way a stepdancer from Margaree will watch a guy from a few miles away move adroitly around the floor and sniff dismissively, "Oh, he's from Inverness," as if that explained *everything*.

Sometimes we even forget our local rivalries and it is just us versus everyone else. American writer Dorothy Duncan couldn't quite figure out the nationality of a man she met on a steamship from England bound for Halifax. "I'm a Nova Scotian," allowed Hugh MacLennan, the Halifax novelist who four years later became her husband. In *Bluenose: A Portrait of Nova Scotia* she wrote: "He hadn't said a 'Canadian' and he obviously didn't think of himself as a Canadian. What could Nova Scotia be like, that its people gave this name to themselves with such pride in their voices that one felt they were convinced of a superiority palpable to the rest of the world?"

This powerful loyalty touches everything. But nothing more than politics, Nova Scotia–style. This is high comedy and low cunning, payoffs and paving jobs, conspiracy and collusion. An old-time whiff of the rum bottle, a timeless hint of Tammany Hall. No different, I guess, from how things were a couple of centuries ago, after London ordered Gov. Charles Lawrence to create a legislative assembly for Nova Scotia. I sometimes imagine how politics was played back then: the partisan county sheriffs who let only voters supporting their candidates cast ballots, the "houses of entertainment" where thousands of pounds were spent plying voters with beds, food and booze, the merchants who jostled for power by forcing their debtors to vote for them, the local heavyweights who simply got together and selected candidates with the understanding that they would be uncontested on election day. "Where elections were fiercely contested, however," historian Brian Cuthbertson wrote in his learned and amusing book *Johnny Bluenose at the*

Polls: Epic Nova Scotian Election Battles 1758-1848, "there could be much fraudulent voting, drunkenness, epic battles to gain possession of the passageways leading up to the hustings, intimidation of voters, and great expense to candidates."

The party in power made no difference. So ingrained was patronage that even Joseph Howe, the champion of responsible government, lobbied for political appointments. When Edgar Rhodes, a Tory, stepped into the premier's office in 1925, he faced a pile of nearly two thousand unanswered letters and telegrams from people looking for work. Some of them read like this: "I am writing you to see if there is any possible chance of your giving me some kind of permanent position this year. There are seven Tory votes in my family, and we have always been good Tories, not people who have turned their coats at every election like some of our Tories in this town whenever they wanted a job. And it is pretty hard on a young fellow to be supporting a government that can't do anything for him." Or this: "I am a poor widow of ninety years of age. I am writing to ask you if you would be kind enough to send me a nice little check to last me through the long, cold winter. I have supported your government in the past." Or the one that came from Dartmouth nearly a year after the election: "As this is 5 June, 1926, I've written your government asking for work and got no satisfaction. This is the last letter I intend writing. Now there are six voters in my home. We all worked and voted for the Conservatives at the last election ... but I didn't work for thanks. I want something for my husband, and if I don't hear of anything from you by the end of next week, I intend to work and vote for some other party that will give us work."

I do not want you to think badly of us. Animals, after all, look at each other a little funny when the water hole starts to dry up. Politics has always been more than a hobby in a place where prosperity, even survival, means allying yourself with the party in power. In Nova Scotia politics makes jobs magically materialize then disappear into thin air. It makes landlords rich and highways appear where only dirt roads once existed. It ruins careers and spawns men who seem stranger and larger than life. And of course it creates theatre—great, great theatre. I left Nova Scotia during the John Buchanan years. From afar I read about MLAs going to jail over expense account fraud, scandals involving mechanized toilet seats, a Halifax building known as the Green Toad and the premier's own blossoming financial problems, which were so extreme that at one point he was living off his credit cards. Buchanan— who once while on the campaign trail declared that "elections should not be fought on issues"—barked like a dog in the historic legislature to silence opposition critics. Then an obscure deputy minister who felt he was the reincarnation of St. Thomas Aquinas— seriously!—sat down at a routine committee meeting and accused Buchanan of accepting kickbacks and directing government contracts to friends and political allies. The RCMP investigated and cleared Buchanan of any wrongdoing. But he was gone by that point anyway, rescued by a Senate appointment from Mulroney like one of the last out from the American embassy in Saigon.

As an interim replacement the Tories chose dairy farmer Roger Bacon, the Yogi Berra of Nova Scotia politics. He was prone to calling life a "three-way street," summing up the problem of unemployment by noting, "If those people weren't unemployed, they'd be working today," and standing before a national TV audience after Buchanan's surprise resignation and saying "we was all shocked." A sane man, he didn't even run for the party leadership. For rebirth the Tories turned to Donald Cameron, a humourless dairy farmer from near Pictou who claimed he would do away with political patronage, then a couple of years later ended up taking, of all things, a Mulroney patronage position as Canada's trade representative in New England.

Which brings us to the here-and-now. In today's Halifax *Chronicle-Herald* I read about the latest on the $200-million originally slated to improve a stretch of highway not far from New Glasgow, which federal public works minister Dave Dingwall and provincial transport minister Richie Mann have shifted to build some new roads in their own Cape Breton ridings. Then I saw the latest installment in the saga of the patronage-swilling grassroots provincial Grits, who are so despondent that Premier John Savage hasn't handed over the usual paving jobs that they're trying to run him out of office. As I put down the paper I was sure that right then somewhere in the province a political IOU was being called, a palm was being greased, a handful of men—and they are always men—were sitting in a quiet room, cigar smoke curling towards the ceiling, forever plotting.

■ ■ ■

I'm into it now—the part of the province that makes Nova Scotia truly and forever New Scotland. Nova Scotia, as I've already stressed, is full of countless life forms. But, up here, along the Northumberland Strait, a kilt is still de rigueur and the pipes assault the senses in stores, malls, schools, just walking down the street. Here the story of the *Hector,* which arrived in 1773 with the first shipload of 180 Scots, carries the same resonance as the saga of the *Mayflower* does in Massachusetts. The destitute pioneers arrived, expecting a land of cleared farms. What they got was a spot with such impenetrable forest that when John MacLean, the most renowned Scottish bard to come to North America, settled at the tiny hamlet of Barney's River in 1819 he called it "a place contrary to nature." In his "Song of America: the Gloomy Forest" he poured out the sorrow and bitter disillusionment he felt at having suc-cumbed to the "tempters" of emigration and their "fables" of life in Nova Scotia. Elsewhere he wrote:

> I'm not surprised that I'm sorrowful
> As my habitation is behind the mountains
> In the middle of the wilderness at Barney's River
> Without a thing better than bare potatoes,
> Before I make a clearing and raise a crop there
> I must uproot the savage forest
> With the strength of my arms; I will be exhausted
> And in a short while an invalid before my children grow up.

Lord, talk about despair. And the feeling lingers. One hot muggy afternoon I sat with Elmer MacKay in a Tim Horton's in the coarse little steel town of New Glasgow. Formerly a federal cabinet minister, he is now a lawyer and runs the family lumber business nearby. He's a well-read, thoughtful guy who sprinkles his chat with quotes from Machiavelli to Casey Stengel. A good person to have a cup of coffee with and discuss the Scottish Highlanders—his own people—who arrived in the late 1700s after the break-up of the clan system. "Highlanders measure wealth not by how much money they have, but by how many people will follow them," he intones quietly. "They tend to be melancholy, because deep down a lot of people did not want to leave Scotland. A lot of what is called Scottish pride is that they do not forget. They have long memories. They remember."

By the time I saunter down to the field in Antigonish they are all here. Or at least they will be before the night is out. Even the people cutting hay in the fields stop everything when the Highland Games begin, because in Antigonish County only two things are really sacred: the Catholic church and their ancestral Scottish homeland. Which makes it entirely fitting that after spending a few minutes down at the field watching some young pipers and drummers going through their paces, I find myself at one of those long church-basement tables in the beer tent listening to a couple of MacDonalds chattering about the church and its troubles. The usual stuff: a bunch of priests being charged for taking liberties with choirboys; the latest foibles of former father Brian MacDonald, who now lives crosstown with his wife, the former Mrs. Conrad Black; the editorial policies of the most magnificently named of all Canadian newspapers, the Antigonish *Casket,* an organ of the local diocese. Everywhere are tartans—Beaton, Gillis, Cameron, Chisholm, MacDonald, Macdougall, MacEachern, MacInnis, MacIsaac, MacLean, MacLellan, MacLeod, MacNeil, MacGillvary. I dodge the dancing kids, step around the old men with the Hiberian visages, leaning on their thick canes, and make my way to the bar for another round. When I return, the MacDonalds—not the D.D.s— invite me back for dinner.

Afterwards the man of the house drives me to the outdoor military tattoo, which for many people is the highlight of the whole event. Lots of gunfire, drumrolls and the peal of bagpipes, which always reminds me of small animals being pounded with mallets. Little girls highland fling upon a wooden stage; great bearded kilted men stride across the grass under the star-filled sky. At a stop sign after the show ends I ask a car full of people for directions. They say get in and drive me through the St. F. X. campus right up to the Student Union Building. Inside a Celtic rock band named Rawlins Cross is in full flight.

They've got two speeds—fast and faster. The effect is a sound so loud that it almost sucks the air right out of your lungs. Ian McKinnon, the leader and bagpipe player, once told me about a tour they made of outport Newfoundland. "Now you have to know that we don't play 'I'se the B'y,'" he patiently explained to the owners of the clubs, Legions and restaurants who booked them. Which was fine until they landed in some hiccup of a place on the Great Northern Peninsula where they opened with a couple of their signature tunes, which fuse rock rhythms with traditional Celtic instruments. A few minutes into the performance a huge fisherman lurched towards the stage, slammed down a hand that McKinnon remembers as twice the size of his own and said through clenched teeth, "Play something I can fuckin' dance to, will ya?" A test of artistic commitment. The boys from Rawlins Cross looked at him, they looked at each other. Then in perfect unison they sang: "I'se the b'y that builds the boat/I'se the b'y that sails 'er/I'se the b'y who catches the fish/and takes her home to Lizer."

Me, I'm enjoying the hell out of it. A woman who reminds me of someone I haven't seen in twenty years dances for a moment in a blue light and then is swallowed by the protoplasmic crowd. The effect is eerie, a momentary crack in time. Like if I scanned the room I'd see me as I looked in '78, perhaps doing the Lowdown, probably wearing army fatigues, hightop Adidas, a checked shirt with the tails out. I might have been with the girl I was dating at the time. For a moment I considered ordering a rye-and-ginger— the drink of the moment circa 1978—to really set the time machine in motion. Then thought about the dangers of adding whisky to a pathetic nostalgia for lost youth. Instead, I order a Keith's and let the sound pour over me.

By twelve-thirty Piper's is wired. I fight my way to the bar next to a Newsworld producer and his Antigonish-born wife who are down from Halifax for the party. "Dennis Hopper," she says.

"Huh?"

"That's who you remind me of. Dennis Hopper."

"She's right," her husband tunes in. "She has this knack for picking out celebrity lookalikes. It's amazing. You really do look like Dennis Hopper."

"He's thirty years older than I am," I protest, not welcoming the comparison.

She shrugs, gets this half-apologetic "I hate to tell you this" smile on her face and says emphatically, "You look like Dennis Hopper."

I slink away, casting dark glances over my shoulder. Then forget about it. Where I am could be Saturday night on the Isle of Skye. Except in the Outer Hebrides there probably wouldn't be as many kilts and as many slurred Gaelic greetings of "Clamar a tha thu?" (How are you?) and "Slalnte" (Health). From the front of the room the lead singer of the house band booms out the last note of "Barret's Privateers," then slides into "Northwest Passage." The dance floor is jammed—boomers, grungers, stepdancing oldtimers, all lost to the moment. There's a primeval feel to the whole thing, as if I've wandered into some primitive ritual viewed by outsiders on pain of death.

About then I recognize another Chisholm, this one a television reporter from Halifax wearing a kilt, pipe band jacket and a Tilley Endurables hat, a souvenir from the Gulf War. In tow is his baby-faced brother-in-law—a new millionaire after inheriting a family fishplant—and a tall guy with a huge head named Cameron, who I gather is some sort of legendary local brawler. Past 1 a.m. now, which means time to refuel. We hop the four-foot chainlink fence in the Piper's parking lot. Chisholm catches a foot near the top and hits the concrete with a splat, but bounces up instantly, like a light heavyweight pretending the knockdown was just a slip.

My notes start to get a little sketchy here. All I know is that we wolfed something down at the sub shop, then headed for the door, Chisholm gimping around like an amputee by now. We cab it to a house party across town. A young crowd, mostly standing around in the kitchen drinking and listening to the band from Piper's, which had magically materialized here. Minutes later I'm in the back of a half-ton, getting a lift to my motel. When I tilt my head back I can watch the inky sky, white pinpricks and the tops of the big elms almost meeting overhead.

My next conscious thought comes when I open my right eye and see the alarm clock blink 8:30. Which means that after watching *The Adventures of Buckaroo Banzai across the Eighth Dimension* on the late show I had something like four whole hours of sleep. I lurch over to the window, open the drapes and shrink from the light like Peter Cushing in *The Horror of Dracula*. It could have been worse. The room is as spare, clean and white as a top-line hospital ward. The windows are open and the wind waving the long valley grass outside keeps the room cool and fresh.

Pay the bill. Down to the field, where the highlight of the competition, the ancient Scottish heavy events, are under way. Men with arms the size of my waist—including one Billy Morse, all six feet and 350 pounds of him, appropriately enough from nearby

Giant's Lake—grunt, yell, then send heavenward big rocks, telephone poles and a nasty-looking thing called the ancient hammer. A behemoth named Harry MacDonald—who, I note from my program, is six-one and 320 pounds and hails from London, Ont.— seems to be grabbing most of the hardware.

A few yards away I notice the Newsworld producer and his wife cowering behind dark glasses, leaning on each other for support. I sneak up from behind, startle them with a lively "Howareyathis-morning," then feel immediately better watching them shake their heads in despair. I buy a big order of fish and chips and eat it leaning on a tree stump that is probably four feet in diameter. I feel full of pep now, spirits so buoyant that even an American tourist a few feet away droning on about his bypass surgery doesn't spoil it.

It is what people in these parts call a big day—a day when you feel kinship with the world and just about everyone in it, including by God the couple from Halifax now in the grip of their awful hangover. On days like this it's hard not to feel the sense of communal loyalty that comes from believing we're all in it together. The principle is unconditional; it applies in good times and in bad. That, I suppose, is the true test of this concept of tribe. If I had any doubt of this it disappeared the moment I left Antigonish. Around here they remember when everything was here, when the place brimmed with confidence, when their farmers were the most productive wheat growers in the province and when their industries—shipbuilding, steel, coal—were the envy of the rest of Nova Scotia.

The scrappy towns and hamlets of Pictou County exist in a knot tied so tightly together that it is impossible to tell where New Glasgow and Stellarton end and Trenton and Westville begin. It's in my mind, I concede, but Plymouth will always be different. Maybe it has always looked as it does today, its streets lined with the tiny semidetached boxes built by the mine companies, and the unemployed miners and pensioners shuffling down the sidewalks. Everyone has been to spots like this: working places where you can't help being reminded that someone else always calls the shots. Here, most of all they remember the day a fireball shot through the Westray coal mine on the outskirts of town, leaving twenty-six local men entombed in the pit. I was in town that day, watching the weeping family members stagger to their cars after learning there was no hope. Four years later I stood by a memorial as some of the same men and women embraced and wept under a powder-blue sky, so different from the wet, grey day when the explosion took away their sons, brothers, husbands and uncles. It was as if time had stood still for them: the bodies of eleven of the men remained buried underground and the answers about who ultimately was to blame for the disaster were no closer.

Again it was just weary, eternally sad people, clinging together in their pain. They looked timeless, as if centuries ago they could have stood in a far-away land, huddled arm-in-arm with the same anguish on their brows. Then, as now, the tribe was the best hope for survival. At the very least it provided a fire to warm themselves against the terrors awaiting in the dark.

Six

Shine

—

DAWN CANNOT BE FAR OFF NOW. IT HAS TO BE NEAR. I HAVE TO KEEP thinking that morning will eventually break here in the woods atop a far mountain in darkest Nova Scotia. All my best instincts told me to be wary of the liquid, clear as nitro, in the plastic two-litre pop bottle. I had been warned about the blind and halt stumbling through institutions across the province after a night spent guzzling this swill. But that is the root of its terrible power. One glass, actually just a finger mixed with a tumbler full of Coke, and I'm carrying on a perfectly lucid conversation. Next thing I know there's this roar of awful accordion music all around me, I'm peering through the cigarette smoke at what looks like a huge dog—a golden Lab who I have to admit can really step out—waltzing on its hind legs with this dangerous-looking character. And a voice, frighteningly like my own, screams "Yessssss, how we love to polka, we all love to polka!"

Just look at this crowd dancing round the kitchen floor: the systems analyst from Halifax, the identical-twin Polish pepperoni millionaires doing the can-can, the mechanic fixated on Dostoevsky; the aw-shucks peacekeeper from the Persian Gulf, the old moonshiner, face-down asleep at the table a few minutes earlier, now performing his strange little jig. Then me, leering like an idiot, helping the others belt out a polka tune as loud as Nazis in a Munich beer hall. It is one strange, strange moment.

"You having a good time, son?" someone yells in my ear.

I just smile as the first shudder of what will inevitably be a monster hangover ripples through my body. The pathetic thing was, I had only myself to blame. No one held me to the ground and started pouring this swill down my gullet. It's just that I've always been fascinated by this inherent underpinning of the Nova Scotian identity—this larcenous streak that just refuses civilizing. Once these shores were haunted with pirates, then privateer boats preying on British vessels, then speedy little schooners running booze for Al Capone's boys, then smugglers running illegal swordfish beyond the 200-mile limit. Onshore we had highwaymen. They disappeared. But the bootleggers in North End Halifax and Sydney's Whitney Pier stayed as busy as ever. As for the moonshiners, they passed along the secrets of their underground art from generation to generation like magic spells. As liquor got cheaper and cheaper it made less and less sense to distill—I use the word advisedly—your own. Yet the stills kept simmering away back there in the woods. Because this was not really about money. Just a small, lovely act of defiance, an unwillingness to accept someone else's definition of right and wrong. A rebel's yell.

Bill, which we will call him because it is not his name, worked with my wife as a systems analyst at a big Halifax outfit. Somehow he learned of my fascination with shiners. Which led me to one of those nondescript spots I've driven by dozens of times. You have to have the right connections to reach here. There are no arrows pointing out the moonshine trail. No tourism department literature trumpeting the stills hidden in the hillside. Never in a million years could I have found my way. But here I was with a bunch of strangers who've taken me in, no questions asked. Probably because once you had an entrée you were *in*. Or as Bill warned: they'd whomp the living crap out of me if I ever squealed.

The five of them do look dangerous and tribal standing around the steel drum with the fire blazing inside as I come to a jerky stop a few feet away. They wear work clothes and stern expressions. One of them, the oldest, is already into the shine. They eye me for a second, then return to their conversation about the Battle of Culloden. Seconds later the talk turns to federal politics before they're onto the information highway. I don't say much, just soak in the conversation, which is as elevated as any I've encountered in a long time.

Suppertime before I realize it. At the old guy's house we pull up chairs to the single biggest meal I've ever seen: steaks, barbecued chicken, coldcuts, a baked ham, a turkey, deep bowls full of mashed potatoes and salads, a couple of pies steaming from the oven, everything washed down with glasses of shine and Pepsi and fruit wine. Normally I'm not much of a trencherman. We're all told that too much food—particularly this kind of food—gives you an ass like a sofa cushion and makes you drop dead at an alarmingly early age; the sheer piggish joy of gorging yourself has become a sin right up there with necrophilia. There is no particular reason why I chose this precise moment to emancipate myself from decades of repression. But I make a fascinating discovery: inside this average-sized body, a fat man has always been dying to get out. No glazed-eyed franticness to my assault on the table. I operate smoothly and methodically as the cook keeps piling more food on my plate. I could just go on forever. When I finally lay fork and knife down and push my plate back in surrender, one of the boys lets out an appreciative laugh like deep thunder. "Christ, John. You sure can pack away some groceries." Blink of an eye I'm holding tight on the back of the ATV, dodging branches and trying to keep my inner organs from being pulverized as we blast up the hill.

These, as I know them, are the facts about moonshining in Nova Scotia: the RCMP has no idea how many stills exist across the province; the ones they do find tend to be set up in basements, woodsheds and forest hollows by men with names like Moonshine Bill and Deepwoods Dave, who use recipes that go back a couple of generations or so. The process is deceivingly simple: start with a liquid base, which can be as fundamental as water, add yeast and sugar. Let it ferment for a week or so until the alcohol level hovers around 17 per cent. Put the mash in a cooker, which could be anything from a steel beer keg to a large tank. Place it over heat and wait for the alcohol—which boils at a lower temperature than water—to form a gas, which is siphoned off and cooled until it distills into a highly concentrated liquid. Then repeat the process.

"It all depends upon how many times you run 'er through," says the elder in the group, a thirty-five-year veteran of the craft whose father, ironically, spent the Prohibition years as a police officer chasing rumrunners in New Brunswick. We are sitting at a rough table in a cabin somewhere in the woods. He's no hillbilly, a retired engineer actually, but like the others seems to revel in the outlaw life. At seventy, he takes pride in his work, distilling his product three times, once using charcoal filters, before deeming it drinkable. "The stuff that only goes through twice can be godawful," he confides, pushing an old two-litre Coke bottle towards me.

The label has mostly peeled from the plastic, as if the contents radiated immense heat. The liquid is as bright as spring water. I undo the cap and lower my nose to the opening. My sinuses are in their usual clogged state. Even so, enough of the fumes seep in to trigger distant memories of being chloroformed as a kid so a gash on my forehead could be stitched up. He produces a tumbler, pours an inch in.

"Cheers," I say gamely.

The others just smile as I take a sip. At a university party back in the days when people actually handed bottles around I once took a haul on a plastic jug and found I'd just inhaled a cup of rubbing alcohol. Immediately I began gasping like a beached carp. Two hours later, my mouth and lips were still numb. I think it was three full days before my tastebuds began to function again. This stuff isn't that bad, even if unconsciously my upper lip begins to curl in revulsion. I manage to croak, "Hey, that's good."

He looks immensely pleased and starts pouring me some more.

Panicking, I try to divert him with a lame question about the Mounties. He waves a hand dismissively. Long as they don't sell to toddlers, or the desperate wife of some shine-addled layabout doesn't blow the whistle on them, he brags, he and his ilk are safe. I'm relieved to see him add a gallon of Pepsi to the glass before handing it to me. There are so many unpaid lookouts in the woods and hills, he adds, that by the time the Mounties got here there would be nothing left but a faint hint of shine in the air. That and the echo of laughter somewhere in the hills.

He leads me into a back room to show me his still. It doesn't look like much: a blackened metal keg, a bunch of bent wires that run to the cool stream out back. You've got to like their spirit. I feel like a member of the James Gang, sitting in this room full of bleary eyes, cigarette haze and hockey chatter where the defiant, irreverent spirit of the outlaw lingers like smoke. I'm giddy as a kid when we pile back onto our ATVs. It's time to ride! I'm without fear now, roaring down the hill to destination unknown. A small detour first to show me some blueberry fields. Bill cuts the engine. "Just look at that sky," he says, tilting his head backwards for a better view of the black bowl dusted with silver. "I come out here sometimes by myself just to see that sky."

I awake with a clear head, just before six-thirty. I hear Bill snoring down the hall. I creep downstairs and open the front door: overcast with mist rising from the grass around the cabin. If my life depended on it I could not retrace last night's steps. I know it happened; in my jacket pocket a plastic cup smelling like a hospital operating room tells me so. I drop it in a garbage can, leave a thank-you note on the kitchen table, back the car out onto the road and make for Halifax.

Somewhere in this mess of tapes, pens, notepads and newspaper clippings on my desk is a photocopy of a page from a book that contains this sentence: "I do not believe I have ever experienced anything more exciting than being on that sixty-foot speedboat on a pitch dark night, with cutters in hot pursuit and powerful search-lights vainly attempting to penetrate our smoke screen ... only a bullet could have caught us that night." The writer was Hugh H. Corkum; this sentence came from his autobiography. The surpris-ing thing was not that he spent a decade working on the Liverpool banana fleet, made up of boats that sat low in the water to avoid detection as they hauled Prohibition rum, whisky and fine cham-pagne from St. Pierre and Miquelon down to gangster speakeasies in New York. For in these parts the time-honoured tradition of run-ning liquor has always been as much a monument to rebellious spirit as a way of putting groceries on the table. What I found most interesting—and why I had copied the page in the first place—is that Corkum, who was thrice arrested for rumrunning, wrote those words in 1989. Just after he had retired from a long, illustrious career as the fabled fishing town of Lunenburg's chief of police.

The photocopy sat there for a long time. Periodically I would pick it up and reread it, just because I found it so odd that some-one could move so easily from one side of the law to the other.

"The old rumrunners were almost folk heroes in the small communities," a man a few years older than me with a reddish moustache and calves like those of a workhorse told me one bright summer afternoon. An acquaintance back in Halifax had put us in touch. Fred Gallup was an RCMP sergeant and a member of the Mountie Coastal Watch program, which meant he had one of the great jobs on the planet. We were in one of those fat rubber Zodiacs, flying across Mahone Bay, hitting the low breakers with enough zip to get airborne for a couple of feet before landing with a small explosion of water.

This is what Gallup and his fellow G-men do: blast at high speeds up and down this riveting coast. Once probably they would have been looking for guys like Corkum. The very landscape—the hundreds of hidden coves, harbours and islands—would have been against them, each bobbing head in a dory a lookout, each schooner blocking the way to port a delaying tactic. But running booze was tradition and beating the system. Drugs, today's contraband of choice, are big money and local kids turn junkies on some far-away Toronto street corner. No one feels much affinity for the South American cartels that discovered Nova Scotia once Washington choked off the drug traffic into the United States. A few locals, needing the cash, hold their noses and play along, acting as mules moving the dope from the mother ship anchored far offshore to land under cloak of darkness. Even they know it is different. There is no pride in it. No panache. Just dirty money. It's not just illegal, it's wrong.

"They dump it anywhere: on a hidden beach, in the woods where a couple of guys are waiting in all-terrain vehicles. They'll find a couple of small wharfs that anyone else would think are no use whatsoever," Gallup says, pointing to a pair of decapitated piers. "Sometimes they're quite brazen about it. It's frustrating. But we have so little manpower there's not a lot we can do. Some people say we get 20 per cent of the dope that comes in, others would say only 2 per cent. It's like squeezing a balloon. Squeeze one part and it just pops out somewhere else."

Yet, despite the immense odds in the dealer's favour, their ships hit ice, they get drunk and talk too much, they draw attention to themselves with their funny accents, flashy yachts or by paying for their clams and chips with a hundred-dollar bill. Or sometimes they panic, like the faint-hearted group who dropped $525-million worth of hash on a secluded beach near the hamlet of East Berlin because they thought a couple of locals rowing by in a dory had spotted them.

Yet they were Pablo Escobars compared with the ones who tried to land 500 pounds of Moroccan hash around here a few years back. Imagine, such lousy sailors that they had to be rescued by the Coast Guard and still couldn't get close enough to shore for the dropoff. Eventually, one of them set out in rubber dinghy; a fisherman found him stranded on the rocks near Port Mouton with a broken toe and, for some unexplainable reason, a guitar strung over his back. By now the Winnebago he was supposed to rendezvous with was gone. He checked into a motel in the area—owned by a retired

RCMP officer—then skipped town, conveniently leaving behind his passport and drawings of the boat, clearly showing where the dope was stowed. It gets even more pathetic: a month later he resurfaced with a partner in an old camper van with a dilapidated boat slung across the roof. The Mounties tailed them to a small cove, watched as they dropped their boat in the water, then shrunk back in disbelief as their engine exploded and went up in a fireball. The pair swam back to shore, hopped dripping-wet into their van, drove a few miles and walked into the thick woods. When they staggered into the clearing, lugging their waterproof bags full of hash, the Mounties were standing there with their cuffs out.

Gallup had cut the engine to tell me these stories. As we sat there bobbing in the waves, another Zodiac, full of Mounties and Revenue Canada agents, pulled alongside. Someone had noticed something strange behind an island on the furthermost end of the Bay.

"Hold on," warned Gallup. "I'm just going to ease this out a bit."

Then, a Miami Vice moment as he pulled out the clutch and we joined them in a tight little formation thundering in tandem eastwards. Ten minutes later we rip between some medium-sized islands, then slow way down. Steering with one hand as he raises his binoculars with the other, Gallup keeps a running monologue as we near an anchored black scow. "Look at that hook on the forward spar, what does he use it for? Does he use it for offloading while at sea? What kind of radar is that at the front? Jesus, is that a seal? No, it's a dog." He pauses. "What's he doing sitting in a cove in the middle of the bay by himself?"

The other Zodiac goes in first, pulling up alongside the boat, the boarding party scrambling aboard. "We can't get you too close in case shit happens," Gallup warns. He picks up his radio and asks for a check on the ship's identification. A crew member, or maybe the owner, walks out on deck. He looks in his thirties, long hair, wearing a black T-shirt and sweatpants. He lights a cigarette, takes a few drags and flicks it into the ocean. A few minutes later a woman's voice comes across the radio saying something I can't make out. "Negative," Gallup mumbles, looking a little embarrassed. "Ah, well." The guy on the black boat, who I guess was just minding his own business, waves at us as we begin a big, lazy arc back in the direction from which we'd just come. It is five minutes before Gallup speaks again.

Last time I drove through Yarmouth I was twenty-two and flat broke, coming back from Boston with a couple of Red Sox games under my belt. I remembered absolutely nothing about the town. But now I can see it's an old place, by North American standards a town of great character. For better or worse, the nostalgic glory of its shipbuilding and shipping heyday—when Yarmouth was the richest shipping port per capita in North America—is what remains locked in place. Recent history has been malicious: the fishery collapsed, a regional airline that used to stop here pulled out, a tin mine closed, so did a textile mill. Now there is even talk about the ferry to Maine cutting back on its trips.

The coffee shop is on a painfully noisy street at the other end of town. The man I have an appointment with is here most days at this time because he drinks a lot of joe and because like all people in unpredictable occupations he treasures ritual of any sort. A friend of a friend told me about sitting with Tom—which, naturally, is not his real name—in this very coffee shop as the Department of Fisheries and Oceans (known locally as DFO) helicopters hovered overhead, searchlights on, scanning the woods for a half-ton of fish carcasses that Tom was thought to know something about. He just sat there calmly sipping his medium double-double just like he is when I arrive. Late thirties, lean and capable looking, a fringe of dark hair hanging over his collar and a lined, weathered face that is starting to show the life. He wears jeans, cowboy boots and a windbreaker. I thought he might be suspicious when I called out of the blue, but he seemed happy for the distraction.

I would love to ask him about life here in the 1950s. But he is way too young to remember when Yarmouth was still the sport tuna fishing capital of the world and teams from Canada, the U.S., Mexico, Peru, Britain, France, Italy and South Africa arrived yearly to chum the waters for those monsters. Tuna are as fickle as they are huge. One day they just disappeared; then, as unexpectedly as they had departed, they returned. Too far offshore for sport fishermen, mind you, but in big enough numbers that along with swordfish and lobster they provide a good living for the commercial fishermen of South West Nova, as this area is known.

Tom used to fish. Now he's really a broker, an intermediary who buys and sells tuna and other big fish and makes money on the spread. "Because of the Japanese market the commercial tuna industry has been going good fifteen, sixteen years," he explains. "In the summer months when the tuna fishery is on, anyone with a licence can make out real good. I wouldn't dare put a figure on it, but if they go out there in the run of a summer they could probably stock a couple of hundred thousand dollars. But it's got to be fresh, it's got to be taken care of, it's got to be handled with care. If you hit your tuna against the curb of a boat or on a pallet it will bruise the meat and that takes away from the price. If it's a good-quality fish, with the right fat content, you get the best price."

He offers to show me around. As we head south from Yarmouth along Highway 103, the Trans-Canada, he makes a quick call on his cell phone, then raises his hand from the steering wheel a few inches to greet an Asian man in a mid-sized Toyota driving in the other direction. "See him? The Japanese buy so much tuna—which is just starting—and herring roe, which is already on, that they send over their own people to bid for it in the auction. In the whole area, there's probably about forty or fifty of them. They rent apartments everywhere down through the Yarmouth area, down through the Pubnicos. They hang out together. They go golfing. They rent brand-new cars. They put a lot of money into here."

I'm struck by the clash of cultures: citizens from the land of the samurai, sushi and the salaryman on the loose in a province where a satellite dish in the yard and a new powerboat in the driveway can be the symbols of true social standing. His cell phone rings and Tom excuses himself. A few cryptic sentences later he's back with me, pointing to a clump of islands a few hundred yards from shore. "These are all the Tusket Islands. It's beautiful out here. It's a real nice place. The lobster fishermen go out and they got nice camps, with everything that you'd have at home—microwaves, cable television, even cooks. A lot of them live there the whole six months, they come home on weekends. Some of the families will go down and stay the whole time."

I knew of the Tusket Islands. When I mention I'd heard there used to be a fair bit of illegal tuna caught around here—and that he had been one of the people at the centre of the trade—an ironic little half-smile played at the corners of his mouth.

"It's gotten so hard now," he says in a weary, resigned voice. "DFO monitors the fish tags more and there's DFO at every airport waiting for shipments to Japan. Plus, you can't maintain the quality. You lose big dollars if a fish isn't up to scratch, a lot of money. So it's not really worth it any more."

What was it like before? I ask. Tom's eyes dart around. He lowers his voice a half-tone. "We used to smuggle a lot of tuna out of here, years ago. I mean just seven or eight years ago, and we used to have a ball doing it. It was all night work. Get them in the middle of the night, one o'clock, two o'clock, off-load them on smaller boats, get them to shore and hide them. We'd hide them in the woods, we'd hide them anywhere we thought we could hide a tuna and not get caught. A lot of people used to use medical stretchers to carry them out and put them in trucks, and off you'd go."

When I ask if back in his smuggling days he ever hid fish out on the Tusket Islands, he shakes his head. "We had a place inland that was fifty miles from any kind of water. We had forklifts down at this place, in this big barn. And this road that went into this camp was like a mile and a half, two miles long. Fuck, we're in the middle of nowheres, the fuckin' middle of nowheres, and we'd slush them, we'd bring our ice down there with the trucks, and we'd slush them. We'd have the forklifts down there to take care of it, to load them, holy fuck, and we never got caught down there and we shipped a hell of a lot of tuna. One day we were talking to this guy who says, 'I see trucks and traffic one, two, three, four o'clock in the morning. They go down there quite a while and then they come back.' That was us, so we abandoned that place."

He laughs when I say it sounds like he misses it.

"Oh, yeah, it was fun. It was cat and mouse. I've never dealt in drugs, or anything like that, but it's probably the same thing. You never knew where they were going to be, the DFO officers, you never knew. Oh, they had them everywheres. You never knew when you were going to get it. I was heading for Halifax one day in this tractor-trailer I drove, and when I got in Clyde River, before Shelburne, I stopped on the side of the road for something. It was so foggy, you just couldn't see the front end of the truck. And I stopped on the side of the road and *bang* out of nowhere this DFO guy came behind me, and I looked in the mirror, and there was three officers coming around the side of the truck."

"Shit," I say, getting into the profane spirit of things. "What then?"

"Well, I put it in neutral when they stopped me. They were

almost at the step of the truck, and I put it in gear and I took off. They said, 'Hold that truck!' I hollered, ' 'Scuse the language, fuck you guys,' and I took off. I shut all the switches off, I shut off all the lights. Two-thirty in the morning. I had thirty-one tuna, thirty-one illegal fish in the back. Fuck, I mean, I would still be in prison right now if they'd a caught me. That was like fifteen tons of tuna in the back. I was headed for the airport, and so I took off, and I shut off all the lights, and I just had the driving lights, and no lights on the trailer, no taillights, no brakes. I was just going."

We both look straight ahead for a minute. I don't know what he's thinking about. Me, I'm imagining this huge rig barrelling through the darkness. I know that was a dangerous, irresponsible, illegal act. But I have to tell you, it makes me feel good to sit here a few years before the new millennium picturing Tom blasting down the highway with the law on his tail. Connected as if by a direct line through time to those pirates, privateers and rumrunners who felt the same need to flout convention, live by their own rules and make their own chances as they went along.

Seven

Whazamattaforu?

—

FAR AS I AM AWARE, MY FIRST SIGHT OF INVERNESS COUNTY ON THE WEST SIDE of Cape Breton Island was in summer 1980. It was such a revelation that words do not do justice. So all I can tell you is where I was and why. To know how I felt you would have to be twenty-four, a night-shift sports reporter at the Cape Breton *Post,* lonely and homesick, living in a converted beauty salon in an ornery industrial town and plagued by insomnia. You would have to have worked a late Friday shift, shot-gunned a draught with a colleague at the tavern across the street. Then, on a whim, jumped in his beater and gunned her. My co-worker sang and played the guitar, so I ended up driving the whole way, high beams cutting through the dark until we stopped in the empty parking lot of the Inverness harness racing track. Somewhere before dawn we gave up trying to sleep stretched out on the car seats. He let me off on the outskirts of town where the highway meets the main road. The surf was just over a small hill. But from there the roar of the ocean sounded far away. Mostly I heard my favourite sound on earth—wind blowing through the tree tops—and saw the sun rise in the bluest sky and turn the road into a silver ribbon. I felt the healing warmth of morning. And I said to myself, as I was given to grandiose statements in those days, "Yes, this is it, bury me here."

This is still one of my favourite parts of the whole province. Even if to get there you first have to go across the Canso Causeway, up a stretch of banged-up road and through some scrubby woods. Hard land for tough people on the run from the Highland Clearances. The woods here once resounded with the ring of the axe, the bells of the oxen ploughing the fields. Now it's been reclaimed by the forest, overgrown with neglect and faded dreams. This is an island where symbols count. So crossing the causeway that connects the mainland to Cape Breton, I take notice as the radio shifts as if on cue from rock and roll to Van Morrison singing some old air and the weather turns from that humid, overcast stuff I hate to a sun-dappled clarity, a nice twenty-two degrees. I doodle with the radio dial. Strange news comes forth: an infestation of flies is being drawn to a community manure pile in Kentville; someone has died in a jet crash near Halifax; a crazy man is loose around Amherst.

A few miles outside the village of Mabou the traffic gets heavier and slower. The first things I see are a white church spire and the side of the Shining Waters Bakery and Eatery, adorned with a big painting of the Juno Award–devouring Rankin Family. The Roman Catholic church and Celtic music—interwoven, inseparable, the island's cultural underpinnings. This is one of those truly blessed spots, like the Mississippi Delta, most of Ireland and just about all of Bali. Short on money and material things but long on verve, spirit and a creative force that is just *there*. This place has soul and rhythm. Just find your *métier,* the scene seems to say, pick up a guitar, a whittling knife, a comb wrapped in wax paper. Express yourself.

So many people seem to find their voice in Nova Scotia. This is the land where Hank Snow, Wilf Carter, Rita MacNeil, Sarah McLachlan, Portia White and Anne Murray sang their first songs. Alex Colville's dark genius matured here. Hugh MacLennan wrote *Barometer Rising,* which ushered in a new era of Canadian litera-ture. Sloan recorded what some consider the best rock album ever made in Canada here. No wonder so many artists from away have discovered the place: writers Brian Moore, Robert MacNeil and Farley Mowat; actors Jack Nicholson, Michael Moriarty and Alan Arkin; composer Philip Glass; filmmaker Robert Frank. There are pockets on the South Shore, say, where everyone seems to be in a country-western band, painting seascapes, creating folk art, build-ing violins or writing plays. In Halifax can be found composers who write concertos about ancient Buddhist legends for Yo-Yo Ma, classical conductors once compared by London music critics to Toscanini and enough indie rock bands to earn Halifax the nick-name Seattle North. And then there is Cape Breton, something dif-ferent altogether.

The signs on the street corners and in the windows of stores and businesses are the first hint. The only areas outside Europe where Celtic languages have been spoken for generations are Welsh-speaking Patagonia and Cape Breton—specifically this end of the island, where they still speak a brand of pure Scottish Gaelic that traces its roots through the original Highland settlers back three thousand years. I take a right at the church, following the sign to Mabou Coal Mines, where the blacktop turns to dirt. I follow it until I'm worried that I've missed the turnoff and pull into a driveway to ask directions. A dark-haired woman with an ironic smile answers the door. When I ask her where Ken Nishi's place is she says something over her shoulder in Gaelic. The answer is equally meaningless to my ears.

"A couple of miles down the road," she says. "It has his name on the mailbox. They are good people. His daughter's married to Jimmy Rankin."

The directions are dead-on. When I pull down the steep incline, Nishi steps waving from the wooden two-storey building with the profusion of windows. He wears a faded green mock turtleneck, carries a cane and, though his parents were from Japan, looks like an older version of Graham Greene, the native Canadian actor. Inside, light floods the studio, catching a sculpture of a horse just right. He introduces me to his brother-in-law, Michio Matsunaga, a slightly built man who wears under his windbreaker a T-shirt emblazoned with a big lobster and a Rankin Family hat on his head of thick white hair. Out of the kitchen walks a short, black-haired guy about my age, wearing a day's growth and one of those standard-issue red plaid hunting jackets.

"John," says Nishi, "meet Jimmy Rankin."

Someone hands me a hefty glass of Scotch. I sit listening to Nishi talk about growing up in Salinas, Cal.—John Steinbeck country—during the Depression. He escaped the Japanese internment camps, but still had a rough time of it in the army. After World War Two he came here to teach art as part of an extension program for an American university. When the course ended he asked a neighbour if he knew of ten acres for sale. The neighbour had 115. Nishi paid $850 for the lot, which wasn't much even in 1949.

"The first six years I came by myself," he says in a quiet, clear voice. "I lived in a pup tent and I'd go off hiking over the mountains, all the way to Petit-de-Grat. I'd arrive and these people would come out to see me, you'd think I was the mayor. I guess they'd never seen anyone living out of a tent before. I'm seventy-nine now. Back when I first arrived I'd go out at night and all you'd hear would be the wind and maybe a horse and wagon on the road up in the back. It's changed. But on a clear night here you still just step out under the stars and look up at the sky and you are just in awe."

The others sit stiffly while Nishi and I talk. I feel I'm throwing their whole afternoon off-kilter. My out comes when he explains that Michio is a singer as well as a haiku poet and the former head of computer operations for the Chicago police department.

"Let's hear a couple, Michio," I say, happily taking the cue.

Having grown up near the Mexican border, he begins with a pair of *AI-ai-ai-ai* caballero songs. Then he morphs into one of those laid-back Dean Martin–style Italian crooners and even throws in a little opera. Rankin reappears with a guitar. Rain begins beating down on the windows and whitecaps mass on the ocean. I turn my tape recorder on, sit back and listen to what I decide right then and there would heretofore be known as the Michio-Rankin Mabou Coal Mines Session.

The older man sets the pace with a stately "Bill Bailey," which he ends by admonishing the title character to "get your toushie back home," a low chuckle and a "yeahh."

"We've got Mary Francis rolling over in her grave right now," he laughs.

"Never been done better," says Rankin as he noodles away on his instrument. " 'Saint James Infirmary,' " suggests Michio, deliberately drawing out the syllables and then adding, "Why don't you do one, Jimmy?"

Rankin clears his throat and says, as if at a school recital, "Saint James." There's a false start as they search for the right key. Finally Rankin's guitar opens with this little blues riff and Michio comes in, correctly, a bit behind the beat. The tempo is just right and the pair sway from side to side as if pulling the melody from the ozone. They play it straight until the last refrain when Michio, with Rankin right there alongside him, ad-libs: "Ahhhhhhh hold the flapjacks/ahhhhhh tofu too/ahhhh hold the soy sauce/whazamattaforu."

When it is over he turns to me and explains in a mock-serious tone: "Whazammataforu. That's kind of remembering our parents, how they used to murder the English language. They were immigrants and we remember them with love and humour," he says.

A deep smoker's laugh rumbles from Nishi.

"What's another tune you got there, Michio?" says Rankin.

"I don't know. You want to do that one 'The Yellow Rose of Texas'?"

"Ah, you know that one, what is it, 'Cindy, Cindy'?"

Is that a C? They try it in D, then in E. Finally, together they start: "If I was an apple hanging on a tree" and run it right through to the final chorus: "Getalong home, Cindy, Cindy, getalong home/getalong home, Cindy, Cindy/I'll marry you some day."

They move into a rocking "Franky and Johnny," Rankin punctuating the lyrics with "yeahs," "uh-huhs," "no, nos" and "yeah, yeah, yeahs."

"Now we're getting a little warmed up," Michio declares at the end.

We're still laughing about some of his ad-libs when Rankin quiets the room with a soulful "Go, Lassy, Go."

"Okay, Michio, one more."

"You want to do 'East Virginia'?" They do, and when it's over Michio says, "You know, it took me six months to get the right inflection on 'daahhling.' "

"Jimmy, do 'Malcolm Murray,' " says Nishi.

He clears his throat, says, "Okay, this one's for Ken," and starts: "Stood a lone man out on the highway/in the blackness on his own/through the wind, rain and fury unfolds the story of Malcolm Murray." A simple song, about death, loss and memory. Darker than most of his writing, maybe more personal too. He delivers the closing lines with the ache of truth: "It's been said out on the backroads, there's a shadow by the light of the moon/never fear, never worry, it's just a memory of Malcolm Murray."

We clap at the end. Rankin asks me if I play anything. I so wish I could have said "Sure" and then demonstrated my mastery of Tuvan throat singing. Instead I meekly reply, "No, and definitely not in front of you." Then a cordless phone rings and the magic is gone. His wife, Mia Nishi, comes into the room. She seems perfectly nice. I persuade them to pose for a picture. The first one is stiff and joyless. Rankin pulls up his collar, mugs for the camera and says, "I'll act like a Cape Bretoner." I plead with them to loosen up. The three men smile. I hit the shutter.

The next night, on the front steps of the Normaway lodge David MacDonald, the proprietor, introduces me to J.P. Cormier, big as a bouncer, with longish red hair and wearing cowboy boots and an ornate mustard-coloured jacket adorned with all kinds of little doodads. Somehow I just knew he was coming off tour with Waylon Jennings, the country-western singer. "Who needs Nashville?" he says between deep drags on a cigarette. "We've got all the music we need right here." To prove it he provides a quick mental tour of the various fiddling styles on the island—Chéticamp, Mi'kmaq, Acadian, Inverness, Sydney, Antigonish, Northern Highlands. "All different. All as distinctive as a signature. My style is said to be partway between Winston 'Scotty' Fitzgerald and Jerry Holland. I don't know. That's just what they say."

This is music that came out of the Scottish Highlands at the turn of the eighteenth century like a wild, melancholy fog. Legends Dan Hughie MacEachern, Winston Fitzgerald, Donald Angus Beaton,

Angus Allan Gillis and Angus Chisholm kept the music alive, playing the fiddle at dances and ceilidhs, composing tunes and patiently passing the sum of their knowledge to their anointed successors. So also did musical vagabonds like Dan R. MacDonald, the composer of more than a thousand fiddle tunes who would just show up at people's doors, trading his wit and genius for a few nights' lodging. For a time the notes grew fainter and also went silent altogether. Now it fills the air. The barn at the Normaway is one of the sacred places. Here, when all things are right, music soars beyond ideas and emotions. Here, if you are so blessed, you may listen to unspoken messages that sound like an eagle climbing through the mountaintops, a whale diving to the bottom of the sea, a river meandering, a heart breaking.

Jackie Dunn, who is launching her first CD tonight, has the right bloodline. Sitting on stage in the Normaway's barn, bowing with her right hand and stomping her right foot madly, she's in good company; Hilda Chiasson, J.P. Cormier's tiny wife, on keyboards, and Dave MacIsaac, an inventive fiddler, guitarist and master of countless other Celtic instruments, picking out the rhythm. "I don't know where they'll put me after I die. But if I can hear music like that I don't care where it is," master-of-ceremonies Archie Neil Chisholm, all of ninety years old, yells from his wheelchair. "Drive her, Jackie. As D. MacDonald would say, that was wicked good."

What a showoffy bunch! A young, dark-haired woman steps onstage and does a dignified little step. Once she leaves, a hefty middle-aged lady jumps up and turns up the heat a notch or two. "That's

Jackie's mom," a man standing beside me up by the rafters says. "She's one of the best stepdance teachers around." Then Spoon Boy takes over. Gerry Deveau of Belle Cote is no boy; he's middle-aged, a steeple-jack I'm told. He also plays spoons. He plays them off his thigh, on his knee, elbow and back of his fist and off his noggin. I'm waiting for the hook to materialize from offstage. Then it dawns on me: I'm in the presence of greatness, of a sort. In the front row, five middle-aged women who have to be sisters sit there impassively, only their bouncing feet revealing their pleasure. A couple of old girls in the front get up and prance around. "Drive 'er, Gerry," yells a young guy over and over again. One of the spoons goes flying into the audience. Deveaux breaks into this strange little jig and the crowd goes wild.

Throughout the concert I catch glimpses of David MacDonald bustling here and there. At intermission he stands still long enough to announce, in a fashion, the other upcoming dances in the area. "Who's up at South West Margaree? The Gabriel? Who's up at West Mabou? Judique? What about Inverness? Anybody know who's at Glendale? Jeez, am I actually going to have to prepare for this?"

For the finale the stage is filled: Dunn, both MacIsaacs, Chiasson and a skinny kid I seem to recognize. Wait one minute, that's the groundskeeper. He must be all of fifteen, can't even grow side-burns. Can play, though. They run through jigs, reels, strathspeys— I have no idea which is which—effortlessly, without a break. From where I sit I see one of Archie Neil's legs twitching as the bows fly. He's clapping madly like everybody else at the finish. Everyone piles outside. A few men stand in clusters in the parking lot sipping from mysterious bottles. I cool off with an Orange Crush and fall into conversation with a couple from some Ontario town. Warm now, with a full moon over the mountains, which seems to perfectly suit their reverie about the big-band dances they used to go to during the war years.

Back inside, Dunn and the others are already at it. The action on the dance floor baffles me: partners divide, come together, parade to the end of the room, then part again—men on one side, women on the other—holding hands and doing these little solos, back straight, head unwavering, feet moving faster than bejesus. Within the discipline of the form there is room for individuality: a shuffle of the shoulders, an elaborate little arm movement or dip of the hips, some flashy footwork—these are the hallmarks of style.

"Basically every little place around here has their own step," explains Jim MacDonald, a thinner version of brother Dave, who works the pop stand. "There's a Whycocomagh Set, a Mabou Set, a Judique Set, a Margaree Set. Every set has three figures—two jigs and a reel. During the jig you just stand there shuffling your feet. The reel is a lot more intricate. But it's still easy: toe, heel, toe, hop, toe, toe," he says, demonstrating. When I look as confused as ever he claps me on the shoulder. "Don't worry. A lot of people just walk through it."

"Oh, I'm not worried," I say. "You won't see me out there. Not a chance in hell."

A whippet-thin teenager materializes on the dance floor floating with startling lightness and speed. Someone tells me he is Joel Chiasson from Chéticamp, maybe the best stepdancer on the island. Cries of "Atta boy, Jo-el" and "Yeeehaw!" carry over the music. When he finishes a cheer goes up, but he's already at the pop stand asking Jim MacDonald, "Ya got any 7-Up?"

By the time I turn back, the dance floor roils with old-timers, high-stepping teenagers, middle-aged ladies in Minnie Pearl dresses. A few feet away I hear a lanky, white-haired senior who looks like he just walked off a golf course say this is the third dance he's been to tonight and the third time he's had to change his shirt. He's right: sweat drips off everybody. I feel a hand on my arm and—oh my God!—Hilda Chiasson is asking would I like to join her in an Inverness Set.

Now, I love music, and am coordinated enough. But when the two elements come together on the dance floor, well, I just don't know, somehow I'm instantly back in high school shuffling like Quasimodo around the gym, certain that everyone in the room is staring gape-mouthed. But before I can think of an excuse I'm out there.

It begins innocently enough. I manage to make it through the promenade part and the spin thing without maiming myself or any of the other dancers. Everyone smiles indulgently when it comes time to switch partners and I end up going in the wrong direction for two choruses before I can get turned back around. Then the reel, when the men and women step back to separate sides, hold hands and solo. This is where you're supposed to break bad. Jim

MacDonald's voice echoes through my head. *You just stand there shuffling your feet.* I try to do it, all right. But what in God's name is happening? I'm picking up speed at an alarming rate, my feet weaving faster and faster, sliding back and forth like, I imagine, a Celtic James Brown. Sweat pours down my spine. I am prancing around on my toes with every muscle in my body tensed, and my calves start to ache.

It's as if I am in some bizarre spirit world—let's call it the Land Without Rhythm, the place occupied by Baptists, Reform Party members and just about every white male who never owned a motorcycle. Where "Shake Your Bootie" is always playing. Hilda, fanning herself with a piece of paper as she floats easily about six feet away, watches with growing alarm. When we come together again she lies badly about how well I'm doing. The tune finally ends and she says something about being warm. "See, nobody was looking at you," she whispers as we head for the sidelines. Hilda, I got news for you!

I stumble towards the pop stand to replenish lost body fluids. The giddy feeling—or maybe it's the sugar buzz from all that pop—is still there a few minutes later, behind the wheel in my car. The fog is so thick that the high beams don't even cut through it. Otherwise not a light anywhere. I realize I am probably lost.

Stands a lone man, out on the highway.

PART THREE

Show Me the Way to Go Home

Be the current against us, what

matters it? Be it in our favour,

we are carried hence, to what

place or for what purpose?

Joshua Slocum

—

Eight

The Last Best Place

—

I CANNOT TELL YOU HOW TO FIND IT, THAT SPOT WHERE THE AFTERNOON LIGHT looks the way you always imagined it should. Where the most heartbreaking strain of music you've ever heard floats from nowhere through an open window at two in the morning. Where your rhythm perfectly matches the ebb and flow of life—as if all along you've been dancing a dance right for just one partner, then turned and saw them at last saunter out into the spotlight. All I can say is that you know when you are there.

I am not talking about the place where you were born. Or the pleasant, pretty and prosperous spot you like to head to when you can dump the kids for a long weekend. What I'm talking about is something totally different. A combination of things, really. Take a bunch of notes and shake them up. They come out one way it's Duke Ellington, another it's Ornette Coleman. Mystery and magic either way. But everyone must find their own way according to their needs and desires. Then maybe you'll make it home.

At least this is my theory. More so now than ever, because I know that in Nova Scotia as the century hisses and clanks to its end I'm not alone. At times it can seem everyone here is from somewhere else. There are new faces, names and bloodlines: Germans, Swiss, Irish, Americans, Japanese, frothy New Agers and hard-headed businesspeople, movie stars, farmers, poets, inventors, carpenters, software designers. Summer people are one thing. The ones who make a bigger commitment—the true come-from-aways—are not here for career advancement: this is still a place that lost its organizing principle with the disappearance of the fishery and the coal mines. So what draws them is something totally different. Something with no relation to real estate prices and the kind of hooey about striking it rich that got the original settlers to Nova Scotia in the first place.

This is not an original thought. Nova Scotia has had a thing about it for the longest time. One day I was in Cape Breton heading inland where water stroked the shore of Great Bras d'Or lake. A partially cloudy day where the sun comes from the sky in weird beams, laying hallucinogenic shapes across the wooded roll of the hills. On an overcast day the land darkens with power and drama, but this afternoon I was engulfed by light and shade, angle and nuance.

I was imagining a day like today, mosquitoes just starting to come up, a man with thick dark hair and unkempt beard standing beside a slim woman with gentle eyes—stone deaf so she couldn't hear the gulls overhead, the loon in the distance somewhere—on the deck of the steamer cutting across the inland sea. Baddeck, the little village where the vessel stopped en route for Newfoundland, was "possessed of a gentle, restful beauty," the woman, Mabel, wrote in her diary. She turned out to be downright restrained next to her husband. When their steamer ran aground after leaving the village, he returned to Baddeck, where he spent the rest of the holiday at a hotel lazing away the days on the big verandah and the cool evenings in a corner bedroom overlooking the bay. From there he saw a massive headland called Red Head and above it the rounded hill, which he christened Beinn Bhreagh, Gaelic for Beautiful Mountain. There Alexander Graham Bell built home.

Nowadays Baddeck is edging more towards Cape Cod than Cape Breton. Jack Nicholson, Paul Simon, Farley Mowat and Billy Joel own places up here. So supposedly does Paul McCartney. The main street has more than its share of chi-chi shops and restaurants—even a spot for a nightcap; the luxury yachts and cruisers, most of them flying the Stars and Stripes, sit motionless on their moorings; a brand-new golf course is being landscaped nearby. Baddeck, with its curious contrasts, has it all. There are the beautiful old clapboard houses and hidden gardens and there are the tiresome T-shirt shops. There is the elegance of the Bell museum and the cheesiness of motels on the outskirts of town. There is the Alexander Graham Bell Club, originally called the Young Ladies Club and founded by Mabel to give the women of Baddeck some mental stimulation, and there are the pony-tailed hippies who came in the sixties and seventies and stayed.

Once there was little more than the view, which prompted Bell to make his famous statement, since reprinted on virtually every piece of promotional literature that has come spinning out of the Nova Scotia Department of Tourism. "I have travelled around the globe. I have seen the Canadian and American Rockies, the Andes and the Alps and the Highlands of Scotland; but for simple beauty Cape Breton outrivals them all." Inventing the telephone made him rich and famous. He was living full-time in Washington then to take advantage of the U.S. patent laws, but he was a Scot from Edinburgh and found the social whirl distasteful and the summer heat intolerable. So Baddeck, with its lovely white-painted buildings, its rugged hills and deep blue waters, must have been a revelation that first day.

The gates to Beinn Bhreagh, the estate he built, are closed to the public, but a good view is possible from the road outside. Having no idea how to describe it, I fall back upon the words of James Lamb, a former naval officer, newspaperman and author who lives nearby and wrote that Beinn Bhreagh is "a marvellous mixture of architectural styles in the Scottish baronial fashion, encrusted with turrets, balconies, stained glass and ivy-draped stonework, and capable of accommodating up to twenty-six people, in addition to a considerable household staff."

This was no summer home. Bell begrudged every moment spent away from Cape Breton. The estate teemed with life—the members of his huge clan, the brilliant young engineers whom he gathered around him to work on his inventions. He played the Scottish laird up at Beinn Bhreagh, rambling through the hills in his tweeds and knickerbockers, fishing from the comfortable houseboat he had built. Usually, though, he worked. Bell was "not a professional inventor like Edison," said notes at Baddeck's truly wonderful Bell Museum, "but a very independent amateur, experimenting for the pure joy of knowing ... [He] was always more interested in possibilities than in realities and tended to lose interest when experiments reached the stage of commercial application."

But Lord, the ideas the man had. No sooner had he arrived than he set about trying to develop a ewe that would bear several lambs at once. At Beinn Bhreagh he explored ways of providing drinking water through condensation and experimented with transmitting sound under water. When President McKinley was shot by an anarchist he developed a surgical probe to find the bullet. (It was unsuccessful.) When an infant son died of a breathing defect he developed an iron lung. He had staff round up the household cats and drop them out of windows head-first onto piled-up mattresses—a practice of which I heartily approve—to test one of his notions that leverage could be exerted against thin air.

Bell was our Leonardo. Here, for thirty-six amazing years, his genius reigned. Nowhere in the world was like Beinn Bhreagh; maybe nowhere before or nowhere since. What amazing things people once saw just living around here. There were days when the skies seemed to magically fill with giant red silk wedges and rings. The kites he used to probe the idea of moving weight through air had names like Diones (Bird of Omen) and were so big that one monster, called Frost King, lifted Neil MacDermaid from Baddeck thirty-five feet into the air at the end of a rope. One day people could have looked out their windows and seen the Cygnet, the largest and most sophisticated of all Bell's kites, being towed by a steamer 168 feet aloft. On February 23, 1909, they could have seen the Silver Dart lift off from the ice of Baddeck Bay, the first aircraft to fly in the British Empire. In the fall of 1911 they could have seen the cigar-shaped hull of HD-4, a hydrofoil he had designed with Casey Baldwin, his surrogate son, thunder down the bay at a speed hitting 70 mph—the fastest man had ever travelled on water.

I checked into a nice room in a lodge across the bay from Bell's place and walked to the café for one of those starry-night-on-the-lake dining experiences. I sat squinting into the darkness up at where I calculated Beinn Bhreagh stood. Everything about Bell appeals to me: the obsessive way he worked until 4 a.m., alone in his study, encircled in cigar smoke, stopping only to tramp through the hills on particularly windy nights, which reminded him of Scotland. The way when a distinguished scientist came to visit they would sit long into the night on the verandah, overlooking the sea, their smokes glowing in the darkness as they chatted. I concentrate hard on the darkness spread out before me, as if the wink of their cigars might still be visible on the far hill. Somewhere behind the gate into the estate is the boulder marking the tombs where Bell and Mabel are buried. In summer the old house still crawls with his offspring. So you get the picture: Beinn Bhreagh is something beyond itself. Something more than money, pleasure or graceful tradition. A monument to joy and life.

Isn't that what these newcomers are looking for in Nova Scotia? Certainly there are few moments as pure or sweet as discovering there is something else. That where you are is not where you have

to be. Harry Taylor came from Maryland. "I worked for NASA throughout my career as a space scientist. I was an explorer, in a sense," he
tells me. A few miles past Yarmouth, I just had to stop the car when
I saw the sign for the Duck Pond Inn, Space Barn Museum. From the
back door walked a white-haired man with a long, sad face alongside
a small woman with a pleasant but distracted manner—Harry and
his wife, Tina. When they lived in Washington he built instruments
that flew on rockets and satellites to study the earth's environment
and observe the planets. Then, though Harry won't go into details,
something happened. "After many years of service and some other
stories that we may not want to get into I was looking for a change
of venue" is how he puts it. "There was big-city sprawl, crime, drugs
and so forth. I was looking for a little more quiet in my work situation due to some disappointments. So we both decided to look
around for a place that we could work on and develop and still have
a relaxed situation."

They looked around the east coast of the United States, usually
finding things too pricey or too crowded. People suggested either
Prince Edward Island or Nova Scotia, so in 1987 they headed for
Canada. When they arrived at the southwest corner of the
province, the fog was so thick that for the three days they literally
couldn't see the water. They took the ferry back to Maine, woke up
the next morning to a gorgeous summer day with the weatherman
predicting a week of it and decided they hadn't given Nova Scotia
a real chance. "That day we got back on the ferry," he says, "drove
up this road and saw this house."

They moved the next summer and spent three years renovating the place top to bottom. I am inside now, walking around the neat displays of space food, space suits, models of space ships and all kinds of other space stuff. We have the place to ourselves today, but bus tours visit, as do classfuls of local students who listen to Harry expound on rockets and space exploration as well as global warming, ozone variation and other things that concern him. "I'm trying to tell a story," he explains to them, "and the story is not just about the past. Most important, it's about the future, it's about where we're headed."

Outside again, Harry tells me that Tina is sick; he is not sure how much longer they will be able to keep the inn and museum operating. "Come again," he says just before I drive away. "Yes," Tina says, waving, "come again."

This hint of mortality hangs over me for a ways. But the more I think about it the better it is to picture them here, where they want to be, finding a new life and meaning at this stage in their lives. Their very presence confirms it: escape is possible. And, as usual whenever my thoughts drift along these lines, I think about this little parable from *The Maltese Falcon*, one of my favourite books and movies. Sam Spade tells about a man satisfied with his well-ordered life who is one day nearly killed by a falling beam. To adjust his life to random possibility the guy, Flitcraft, leaves his well-ordered existence behind and sets up a new life, which in time becomes just as ordered as his old one. "But that's the part of it I always liked," Spade explains. "He adjusted himself to beams falling, and then no more of them fell, and he adjusted himself to them not falling."

A brighter person, no doubt, would take something different away from that little yarn. Me, I've always been stuck on the thought that reinvention, for better or worse, is possible. A piece of wood falls and a man trades in the shirt and tie and becomes an aromatherapist in Alaska or a boccie hustler in Naples. I've never felt the need. But if the time comes I won't have far to go. Up the coast a way on the Northumberland Strait, where the waters of the Atlantic suddenly grow warm and redemption and change both seem possible. Up here mob wise guys morph into landscape painters, 'Nam draft dodgers blossom into newborn capitalists. Commie-lovers like local boy Cyrus Eaton—the industrialist who made and lost a couple of fortunes in the United States, was excommunicated for his ties with the Russians, then got the bright idea for a thinkers' conference on world peace in the village of Pugwash, which spawned a Nobel Prize–winning anti-war movement—are transformed into heroes.

In winter this can be a hard, unforgiving province. But in August, when the plants are full and the sky is clear and uninfluenced by haze, I find it a liberating place. Things seem to give off the loopy weirdness that surfaces when people are able to live life as they take it. It happens even in the most ordinary place. Wolfville is one of the prettiest of Annapolis Valley towns. It is gorgeous, in a way that touches something strange beneath your breastbone. A sense of the bittersweet lingers. Even if you've never been here before, Main St. is as familiar as a Frank Capra set piece: one of those great old movie theatres, nice-looking restaurants and coffeehouses, comfortable elm-shaded houses, all with the dramatic Minas Basin and lush farmland as backdrop. Once you see Acadia University, the town's tiny perfect Baptist college, you understand why anyone who ever went to school here looks back on their years with a golden hue. I have no idea what it is like inside the classroom, but it seems entirely reasonable that a person could spend a lifetime trying to rediscover the immense joy they experienced here, and probably never find it.

But whenever I visit I'm on the lookout for the straight-backed military bearing, the austere crewcut and the angular, arrogant face of a monk from some superior order. Alex Colville, the man European critics have called the most important realist painter of the twentieth century, lives down Main St. past the university gym in a comfortable house where his wife, Rhoda, grew up. The couple moved here for good after Colville resigned his university teaching post in New Brunswick to paint full-time. "People thought what I was doing was just crazy," he said the one time we met. "Everyone was doing Jackson Pollock and all that crazy abstract stuff. Most of them thought I was just too dumb to know what was going on. But I've never had that much interest in what other people were doing."

I love his work—dark, enigmatic, with the quiet ring of destiny far in the background. As much as that I love the fact that he chooses to do it here. In the very midst of all this beauty and *Goodbye, Mr. Chips* nostalgia so far away from the centre of the art world is Colville, going his own way, ignoring convention, painting trucks, boats and trains, women who bear an uncanny resemblance to his wife and haunted-looking men who seem undeniably like himself.

Bear River, which sits pleasantly nearby in a small valley, its old, roomy wooden homes half-obscured in the heavily treed hills leading down to the cleft that forms the centre of town, is a different kind of place. Some promotional wiz has nicknamed it Nova Scotia's Switzerland. It is quite a sight, particularly when the river that bisects the village is at low tide, leaving the rear ends of the waterfront houses and buildings suspended on timber stilts twenty feet from the muddy bottom.

Visit the local tourism office. Inside, a cheery university student tells how the town was founded by British Loyalists and the German mercenaries hired by the British crown during the American Revolution. Buy a couple of postcards, maybe the one that shows the 1902 Cherry Carnival, which, she says, is still running, even though the cherry trees around here are all gone and they have to import fruit to keep the tradition alive; the other is a tall-masted ship passing down the river during the village's heyday in the Golden Age of Sail.

Bear River clearly isn't doing too bad. Even someone as untutored as me can tell the stuff for sale in the shops and galleries on the main street is made by real artists. The village is getting a name with the tourists. Meantime, every hippy in the world who can still walk has somehow heard about this place—the dog groomers from Vancouver, the woodworkers from New York City, the stained-glass artists from Argentina. Bear River is one Love, Peace, Marijuana, Kill the Pigs kind of place. I like the fact that oddballs flourish here. Bear River, despite its combination of come-from-aways and old-time Nova Scotians, works. I realized this on my first visit after watching a tourist nearly run down by a middle-aged man with thick glasses. He drove an old one-speed bicycle but made the gear-shifting noises of a five-speed mount somewhere deep down in his throat. "Oh, that's Walter Wamboldt," chuckled Rob Buckland-Hicks when I described what I saw. "He's the sweetest guy. He knows the birthday of every woman in town, and leaves them wildflowers on their doorstep." Buckland-Hicks sports a walrus moustache and leather sombrero to go with his Brit accent. He has another nice story: years ago while living and painting in England he came to visit Nova Scotia and ended up spending a few pleasantly aimless days on nearby Brier Island. One day he was lying on a beach on the secluded back side of the island when he looked up and saw a beautiful dark-haired woman wearing a hat adorned with eagle feathers emerge from the fog and walk towards him. He sat there transfixed as she strolled past as if in a waking dream. He spent the next few days hunting her down, ended up marrying her and settled in Bear River, where he runs a choice gallery that handles mainly the works of local artists.

Things like that actually have a chance of happening in Bear River. The last time we were here I took Belle, Sam, and a couple of cousins into a shop called Return of the Toymaker. Inside the toymaker himself leaned over a flywheel drill press, working on a piece of wood. He learned how to make handcrafted wood toys from a traditional German toymaker. When I ask what brought him here he said, "When you follow your heart you know things are right even if you don't know why."

Sometimes I am not sure if I am in modern-day Canada or not. Around the edges of the province it can be hard to tell. In the northeast I once stood in a recreation centre watching twelve hundred Germans who lived in the area belting out Bavarian drinking songs till the little hours of the morning. Another time, outside of the town of Inverness in Cape Breton, I stopped in a clearing on the ocean side of the road when I noticed a cairn. The plaque read: BUAIDH NO BAS (Erected in memory of our MacDougall forebears who settled these shores in 1808 and also their descendants who worked this soil and also those whose blood traces from here).

I am no stranger to this part of the province, where my aunt and uncle summer in a cedar home surrounded by wooded hills, not far from a beach complete with a 100-foot waterfall. But I had never before been to the circular stone and glass house where Sylvia Fischer lives. When I arrive she introduces me to her sister and niece who are visiting, then makes tea and brings out some cookies. She is in her sixties, has short grey hair, a friendly open face and wears an untucked plaid shirt that dangles over black pants. She talks about how her friend Jean, who lived down the way, first came to Cape Breton on a bicycle trip in 1940 and promptly fell in love with the place. And how a year or so later Fischer received an invitation to come down from Chicago and visit. "We came the week the Canso Causeway was built," she recalls, referring to the historic day the island was physically connected to the mainland. "We were the only car on the road, and the first thing we ran into was a flock of sheep. Flowers grew right down to the edge of the road, borders of daisies and buttercups. For the first few years here we lived with Jean in her stable. Finally we said, 'We love it so much we want to stay.' "

Near the door I notice a collection of curled-at-the-corners black-and-white snapshots—fishing boats, rugged faces and some views of the local terrain, all held on the wall with thumbtacks. Fischer says, "All those people used to live up here. Duncan Rankin went to work as a stevedore in Dartmouth; Joe Rankin used to tend his sheep. That's the Port Ban beach down by your uncle Earl's. There used to be two or three fishermen who fished out of there. There used to be fifty people living on top of the cape."

I knew the story afterwards. The mine opened up in Inverness, the people left, the properties sat vacant. Eventually the county sold them off for back taxes. Most went to Americans, but a lot were taken by people from Ontario and elsewhere in Canada. The faces changed. Word got out and the area became a mecca for come-from-away artists and anyone else looking for a beautiful place without distractions where they could do their own thing. I'm told the attendant at the gardening centre at the Co-op is as good at watercolour seascapes as at building a mulch pile. I know of a fisherman who is as likely to be found sculpting in his studio as tending to his lobster traps. Go to a square dance here and you can run into Philip Glass, the composer, or his buddy Rudy Wurlitzer, the screenwriter, or Helen Tworkov, the editor of *Tricycle,* a worldwide Buddhist newspaper published in New York. Take a stroll on the beach and you might end up lending your snorkelling gear to Spalding Gray, the monologist. Or you might say hi to someone, then realize it was Willem Dafoe, straight off a Hollywood set.

Somewhere you might even run into Robert Frank, the reclusive Swiss photographer, filmmaker and spiritual godfather to the New Yorkers who have discovered Inverness County. Now seventy, Frank has lived in Mabou Coal Mines with his artist wife, June Leaf, for the past quarter century. They came in 1970, twelve years after the images he brought together in *The Americans* changed North American photography forever. Moving to Mabou didn't slow him down one bit: he made a film, *Candy Mountain,* about a fellow (played by Tom Waits) travelling around rural Cape Breton in search of a legendary guitar maker (based on Otis Thomas, the backwoods Stradivarius who lives near Baddeck). And, of course, he took pictures. As a *New Republic* review of a retrospective of his work pointed out: "After the death of his 20-year-old daughter Andrea in 1974, the terrain became the correlative of his internal wound, the rocks and pilings and glaciers appearing as emblems of his grief in the many pictures connected to her memory ... The pictures made in Nova Scotia before her death assemble a difficult beauty from bleak elements; in those afterward the bleakness itself is the beauty which emerges pure from surfaces laden with verbal and textural scars."

Since I'm Earl and Rea's nephew, Sylvia agrees to make some introductions on my behalf. She calls a neighbour, Richard Serra, the mercurial, world-renowned American sculptor whose works can be as big as skyscrapers. She puts the phone down laughing. "Big frosty silence when I asked if you could come over. I'll call Joanna," she says, referring to JoAnne Akalitis, the former artistic director of the New York Shakespeare Festival. Akalitis says, "Hey, how are ya, sure, c'mon over this afternoon."

A little later I am inside her bungalow—grey weathered cedar shingles, big windows and an aqua blue metal roof. She has served up iced tea and tasty leftover pasta with eggplant. We eat in a big airy kitchen with funky art posters covering the walls and books scattered everywhere. She's busy: adapting Strindberg's *The Dance of Death* in collaboration with Philip Glass, her next door neighbour and ex-husband, and working on a jazz adaptation of Michael Ondaatje's memoir *Running in the Family*.

"I've been coming here for twenty-five years," she explains between bites. "Phil Glass and I had to get out of New York one summer. We meant to stop in Maine, but I don't know, I guess we just kept on going until we reached here. The fact that it is exactly 1,000 miles away from New York, or maybe it's 999 miles or maybe it's 1,030 miles, that means something. It is a place which has tremendous power. When I think of Cape Breton I think of Paul Bowles who went to Tangier and all those people who visited him like Truman Capote, Tennessee Williams and Allen Ginsberg. They never managed to make a community there, but Bowles stayed. There was no opera, there was no ballet, there was no library with incredible books. But it was to his tastes.

"I don't even really like the country—it's kind of scary for me. But this place is very interesting. Great walks. You can go to a dance. As long as I can swim and go for a walk I'm happy. My best friend here is a priest, Stanley MacDonald, who lives in Sydney. He's got a cottage over there. This combination of woods and sea is great. New England is beautiful, but Cape Breton has an openness that reminds me of Northern California. I also think Nova Scotia is very spiritual—it is no accident that all those Buddhists in Pleasant Bay ended up here. And the culture ... I went to this dance at Southwest Margaree and saw Ashley MacIsaac and said, 'Wow, this is the real thing.' "

A couple of years ago she brought the young fiddler to New York to cast him in her production of Georg Büchner's *Wozzeck*. The setting was nineteenth-century Germany, but under Akalitis's direction it was transformed into modern-day Cape Breton and launched MacIsaac's international career. Nothing unusual in that; her work is shot through with the island's influence. Twenty-five years ago, she and Glass started the Mabou Mines theatre group, which is still going today in New York and is the oldest collaborative theatre company in America. They rehearsed the first piece right here on this property. Later she did Samuel Beckett's play *Cascando*—Glass wrote the music for it—and set it in a Cape Breton farmhouse with a bunch of people sitting around a table. "There were guys with hats and there was this pregnant woman." She laughs. "I thought it was very beautiful actually."

I can't necessarily envision her sitting down to play cards with some of the local ladies and asking if they are up for a round of iced lattes. But accommodation is made all the way around up here. Amusement may skirt the edges of a generational Cape Bretoner's face when a gaggle of New York hipsters troops into the Ceilidh Café, resplendent in their goatees and body piercings looking for all the world like any second now the door would swing open and Kerouac and Cassady would glide through. But even the come-from-aways know that when they arrive in the spring the shopkeepers will wave in greeting. Their neighbours will come to the door and say, "When did you get home?"

Back in town it is midafternoon. Prom dresses are here! says the sign on the bulletin board at the Inverness Small Animal Clinic. In God We Trust, declares the motto for the Evans Coal Mine. From Main St. the beach looks empty and wild. On each side of the road, mine company buildings lean and slump. With time to kill after my visit with Akalitis I stop at the spiffy new offices of the Inverness *Oran* (weekly circulation 8,000, nearly 2,000 of them off-island). Frank Macdonald, bald-headed, wild-bearded, the paper's most popular columnist, is so welcoming that two minutes after meeting him I'm down in the basement enjoying a cup of tea. Macdonald is a wealth of island info and gossip. I'm curious what he thinks about all the newcomers buying up properties, and whether he is concerned that everyone arriving in search of their Last Best Place could ruin the very thing that drew them here.

"Oh, it's not an issue yet. I think part of it's that this area has really started to gain confidence in the last twenty years. You used to hear about Scottish fiddlers. Now they refer to them as Cape Breton fiddlers. There is a new confidence in our own culture rather than simply seeing it as borrowed from something else," he explains. "So far there is nothing to be alarmed about, but a lot to be alert for. We hope we can keep the water slides off the Cabot Trail. We realize this could turn into Disney Land with kilts if we don't watch out."

He has to get back to this week's column. On the way out I grab the latest copy of the *Oran*, which I take the time to read leaning against the car: last week Inverness County council was preoccupied with why the streets of Mabou hadn't been repaired for this year's ceilidh and with formally adopting the daisy as the official flower of the county. There's a long story about a Gaelic summer camp for kids; a piece about a break-in at the Aberdeen electrical station, which urges the culprits—who may have received electrical burns—to see a doctor because "electrical burns may seem to be minor, but in fact they are usually worse than originally perceived." There's an item on a school reunion during which the alumni reminisced about "school fights and black eyes and broken hands." There is an ad for a chemical-free see-through shirt, which covers the entire upper body "to protect against all biting insects; black flies, mosquitoes, tics, no-see-ums." I see notices for Lewis and Marion MacLellan's fiftieth anniversary in Dunvegan. I learn that $30,000 would get you 150 acres in Little Narrows, that the DeVries family had arrived from Montreal to open their cottage, that Mrs. Agnes Dennis of Orangedale and Mrs. Catherine Cameron of Whycocomagh had recently turned ninety, that Malcolm MacKay of the Ottawa area enjoyed "mackerel, eels, gaspereau and home-made maraghs" on his recent visit to the area and that a lady's watch and pair of glasses had recently been found on Inverness Beach.

It reads like a poem about an imaginary place, where time stands still and the world is unsullied and pure, calling to restless souls as if from a dream.

Nine

Big Dreams

—

THERE IS ONLY ONE WAY TO GET TO BRIER ISLAND BY CAR: DOWN A TOUGH, heavily treed strip of land about twelve miles long and half a mile wide known as the Digby Neck. It demands commitment, particularly on a gloomy, sour day when the wind churns the rain into a grim froth that makes the inside of my car seem like the last hospitable place on the planet. I have to wait a few minutes with seven other cars to board the small ferry across to Long Island. Then it's just a short hop to a little spot called Freeport and the second ferry ride across to Westport, Brier Island's sole town.

Here the land ends. It's a magnificent, brooding, Gothic place. Which pleases me to no end. For this is how I always pictured it: fog-bound, battered by wild seas that smash against its step-like cliffs. Brier, I know, is a magnet for violent electrical storms, for bald eagles, ospreys, great blue herons and other migratory birds, for the humpbacks, finbacks and other endangered whales that breach in the waters nearby. This is the Graveyard of Fundy, a treacherous spot where too many vessels to count went down.

I went to Brier Island because of Joshua Slocum, even though I knew he was no saint. Definitely a pervert, probably a sadist, maybe a murderer. And Lord, he looked the part. He peers haunted and dangerous out of those old photographs, like a Bible prophet or the perpetrator of some awful crime—his gaunt face all sharp bones, wrinkles that look like they've been carved with a knife and El Greco eyes forever lifted to the horizon looking for sin. The time I'm interested in was before the alligators came. When he was nothing but a middle-aged failure, a near-derelict with no possessions to speak of other than the once-dilapidated, century-old oyster sloop he found sitting in a Massachusetts farm pasture and rebuilt plank by plank. Slocum got some bad directions from a fisherman as he made his way from Boston to his old home on the northeast tip of Nova Scotia in the summer of 1895. When he manoeuvred the *Spray* into dock at Westport he was technically completing the first leg of his three-year, 46,000-mile odyssey. But the idea of sailing around the world by himself was no doubt hatched here, watching the great vessels move by during the long hours he spent driving wooden pegs into the thick soles of hand-made fishermen's boots at his father's bootshop. So it is no liberty to say that Brier Island is where the great adventure began.

I feel thrilled a century later to stand at the far end of Westport, in front of a small bronze plaque bearing his likeness atop a pile of beach stones. I read his book *Sailing Alone Around the World*— one of the greatest of all adventure stories—years ago but only now finally had a reason to come. Tightly packed near the centre of the harbour, the foundations of its oldest houses dug into the side of the hill, still exposed to the grandeur of the elements, the village seems eerily isolated. I feel alone here at the water's edge, even with a couple of tourists from Saskatoon, also paying homage at Slocum. How, in God's name, must he have felt setting off from here to try to become the first person to sail around the globe singlehandedly, in a boat not appreciably bigger than my Toyota Corolla? In his book he sounds chipper and confident—maybe because he was a desperate man with nothing to lose, maybe because he was a bit insane. Pure, undiluted courage is not something with which I'm well acquainted; I feel brave ordering a dish with three chili peppers beside it on a Szechwan menu. What he did is so startlingly amazing, so far beyond my frame of reference.

It does not surprise me that he began here, in the province where he was born "in a cold spot, on coldest North Mountain, on a cold February 20." For there has always been a frontier feel to this, the oldest place on the continent. Once you hit here you're out of room; there is nowhere else to run. So, along with the decent, hard-working folk, Nova Scotia has always gathered every sort of migrant, hope chaser, roughneck, trickster, incompetent, misfit and failure. It is a place for Big Dreams in all their forms. They are starker here and often more perverse. Just because in such a place they have to be.

Know this about Slocum: he was just sixteen when he shipped out in the British merchant marine, and twenty-five when he walked the quarterdeck of an American coaster as captain. His honeymoon was a voyage to the salmon-fishing grounds off Alaska. Most of his children died at sea. So did his first wife, as their ship lay in the Plata River off Buenos Aires. He married a cousin, Henrietta, from Nova Scotia. On one of their first voyages together, back to South America, the crew mutinied and Slocum had to shoot one crewman and wound another. On the same voyage the crew caught smallpox and the ship, whipsawed by crosswind and currents, broke up on rocks, leaving the Slocums stranded in a foreign land. Salvaging what he could, Slocum built a shelter for his family on the beach, which is where they lived for the five months it took him to build a thirty-five-foot "canoe" he christened *Liberdade*. They needed fifty-five days to cover the 5,500-mile voyage home.

They ended up in Boston, broke with no prospects when a sea captain friend offered to give him a "ship" that needed some repairs. First time he saw the derelict oyster boat lying in the pasture he thought it was a joke. *Spray* was inscribed upon her faded nameplate, but her age and parentage were doubtful. It took him thirteen months to hew the timbers and put the planks in place, to tar and paint the exterior. The job cost him $553.62. When he launched her in April 1893, Slocum wrote, "She sat on the water like a swan." Returning to Westport two years later, he reminisced how he and other boys used to hunt on dark nights for the skin of a black cat to make a plaster for a lame man. And he recalled Lowry the tailor, who enjoyed his tobacco and was also fond of his gun, a combination that was almost the end of him when "in one evil moment" he put his lit dudeen in the coattail pocket where he carried his loose powder. He stayed long enough to overhaul the

Spray once more, "then tried her seams, but found that even the test of the sou'west rip had started nothing." After a couple of false starts, his log for July 2, 1895, read: "9:30 a.m. sailed from Yarmouth. 4:30 p.m. passed Cape Sable; distance, three cables from the land. The sloop making eight knots. Fresh breeze N.W." He was fifty-one years old with only a tin clock for navigation. He planned to circle the globe heading eastward. But in Gibraltar, he heard about pirates in the Mediterranean and backtracked to South America. To avoid going around Cape Horn, he tried to cut through the Strait of Magellan, only the worst sailing waters in the world. After seven attempts and more than two months he finally broke through to the Pacific, shouting "Hurrah for the *Spray*" to the seals, seabirds and penguins. From there he headed for the Samoa Islands, where he met the widow of Robert Louis Stevenson. Reaching Australia, he dropped anchor and stayed for ten months. He resumed his course across the Indian Ocean to the tiny island of Mauritius and then on to South Africa.

He sprinkled carpet tacks on deck before he slept and awoke to the screams of pirates who crept aboard in the dark of night. He nearly drowned trying to free his vessel from a South American sandbank. Stricken by food poisoning and lying delirious in bed, he once saw the ghost of the pilot of Columbus's ship the *Pinta* at the *Spray*'s wheel. But he kept going. "I felt a contentment in knowing that the *Spray* had encircled the globe," he wrote after crossing his boat's outward-bound track. At 1 a.m. on June 27, 1898, he dropped anchor at Newport, R.I.

■ ■ ■

It's spitting rain as I drive along a battened-down main street and pull up to one of the few modern-looking buildings in town. Inside is a gift shop and well-stocked general store as well as a place to sign up for a whale-watching cruise. A slim woman behind the gift-shop counter, with dark hair and high cheekbones, tells me I've missed the last one today. I just snap my fingers, grimace and say, "Dammit."

Her name, it turns out, is Judy Joys. She tells me R.E. Robicheau Ltd., her father's store, used to be located across the street. But that was before the Great Groundhog Day Storm of 1976, with its tidal waves and 130-mile-an-hour winds. Raymond Robicheau was working in his office when a neighbour ran in, grabbed him by the front of the shirt and started hauling him towards the back door. They had just crossed the street when the wall of water struck, blowing out the front of the building, leaving the rest to collapse and disappear in the wake. Joys was living in Vancouver when the big wave hit. So she only heard second-hand how her sister ran down with their father's old army rifle to scare off looters. And how the townsfolk later showed up with money they owed her father, even though all the store's IOUs were washed away in the storm.

The rain keeps the tourists away, giving her time to lean her elbows on the counter and tell me about how wonderful it was growing up here. She tells me about the 6 p.m. curfew for the last ferry run of the day from the mainland and how her family left their house unlocked, even for the two or three weeks they were away on vacation. She talks about the old characters who sat on the wooden bench by the pot-bellied oil stove in her father's store. Over there would be kind-hearted Franky Buck, who was bent permanently double, legend has it, after contracting syphilis as a young man. He committed suicide in his eighties by walking off the end of a wharf. Next to him most days was Ace MacDormard, his face browned and wrinkled from decades on fishing boats, hand-rolled cigarette stuck permanently to his lower lip. Ole Ace had incredibly bad luck: a son and two nephews who died at sea, a house that burned to the ground, a boat that went up in flames and another that exploded while he was gassing up, blowing him onto a nearby wharf. But in his eighties the old roué was still donning his reflector sunglasses, hopping behind the wheel of his huge gas-guzzler, which he had painted royal blue with the same flat gloss that he used on his boat, and taking the ferry to the mainland to visit one of his girlfriends.

She laughs a nice laugh when she tells that story. I get the distinct impression that the isolation here breeds quirk rather than insularity and that eccentricity is more a comfort than a threat. Slocum himself had shot two mutinous seamen, been fined $500 by a New York court for putting one of his officers in irons for fifty-three days and charged with indecently exposing himself to a twelve-year-old girl who had visited the *Spray* while he was docked in New Jersey. But no one batted an eye at the turn of the century when Slocum returned to Brier Island to write his great book about his voyage. Some one thousand people lived here then, including Capt. George Clements Sr., who thought he could rid the island's gardens of insects by bringing toads and snakes from the mainland and shipping over a pair of young alligators he found on a Florida hunting trip.

Nowadays, Joys tells me, the local population shrinks to three hundred during the winter after the cottage owners have gone home and tourist operators close down. Small as it is there remains a tolerant live-and-let-live attitude here. For proof I need only cast my mind to the writer and newspaper editor from the island who left her lighthouse keeper husband not because she found life here too isolated—which *might* have been a scandal—but because she had fallen in love with Allan Legere, the New Brunswick serial killer. Her husband took her back after the zip went out of the romance. On Brier Island nobody excommunicated the woman; they just give a bemused little shake of the head when they tell the story. It really is that kind of place.

So my eyes are peeled for characters as I wander into the tourist bureau and note that 119 people visited there yesterday. Bent by now on a late lunch, I head for a small spot, the back of a house really, a few streets from the waterfront. I have a nice view of the harbour through a window. The young waitress sits at a table watching a soap opera. The cook—early twenties, I would say, wearing a soiled white apron—joins her. Instead of ignored, I feel tranquil as the rain drains from the sky and I sit in the warm room. I order a cheeseburger, cup of coffee and a piece of pie. Then I open Slocum's wonderful book, published when he was sixty-five, nine years before he cast off the *Spray* from Tisbury, Mass., began sailing southeast into strong winds bent for South America and was never seen again. And I read his final written words:

"I learned to sit by the wheel, content to make 10 miles a day beating against the tide, and when a month at that was all lost, I could find some old tune to hum while I worked the route all over again, beating as before. Nor did thirty hours at the wheel, in storm, overtax my human endurance, and to clap a hand to an oar and pull into or out of port in a calm was no strange experience for the crew of the *Spray*. The days passed happily with me wherever my ship sailed."

That is the point, isn't it. People like Slocum are haunted wanderers, constantly moving on to the latest doomed quest. The dream is the thing. The dream is where their spirit discovers itself and acquires the ability to overstep time and space. Slocum and his like need a canvas big enough to paint the grand narrative of their lives. They are looking for a wilder ride—to grip with one hand while the other flails the air like a bronco rider's. To whoop and holler while the rest of us mumble "hip-hip, hooray." To rocket across the firmament in a blinding blaze while the rest of us fizzle and pop.

The guy with the lock-picking tools first told me about Fred Lawrence. We were in Dingwall, a little last gasp of a place at the north tip of Cape Breton. And I had locked the keys in our rental car. My sagging spirits rise a touch when I notice this happened often enough that the inn where we are staying owned a lockjimmying tool worthy of a Detroit car booster. But it proves useless on our missile-proof rental Grand Am. Blessedly it took only a few minutes to hunt down a service station in Neils Harbour still open this late in the day. Half an hour later the overalled garage owner gets out of his truck and unrolls his tools like a surgeon. And as he methodically picked the lock, we somehow got on the subject of Fred Lawrence, who lived in nearby Bay St. Lawrence.

This is one of the truly forgotten corners of the province; the big, brooding landscape looks like it is straight out of *Dracula;* we are the only car on the road for miles. Bay St. Lawrence turns out to be an industrious little place. Even back in the 1930s, when there was no cash around, everyone had a farm and would trade eggs for tea and sell lambs to cover their taxes. Barter gradually gave way to a cash economy when a lot of Bay St. Lawrence men went to work at the gypsum quarry, which opened in nearby Cape North. Things got rough when the quarry closed. But Bay St. Lawrence went from being one of the poorest places in all the Maritimes to one of the most prosperous after the 200-mile fishing limit was established and the local crab fishery took off.

For some reason virtually every scrap of ground in the village has its own place name. Approaching town as we are means passing through St. Margaret's Village, named for the huge Catholic church. From there the road passes a wharf, the credit union and the high school before reaching the eastern edge of the shallow harbour, known as the Pond. Since the highlands circle the town the effect is bowl-like and seems to magnify the effect of the wind that blows like hell off the ocean. Whitecaps—Belle calls them seagulls—top the water. We pull up to a fishing boat in drydock, turn down the Ray Charles on the tape deck and ask a thick-bodied man perched precariously on a ladder if he knows where Fred Lawrence lives. He grunts "Slocum, eh?" and sends us up a dirt road past dozens of lobster traps sitting in a neat pile.

We stop in front of a roomy, grey-shingled house with blue trim around the windows. One wall is decorated with a bone-white arc about fifteen feet across, which turns out to be a whale's rib. There's a basketball hoop at the end of the packed-down dirt drive, a garden to the right and, off to the left, a shed bearing the name Lawrence. Inside, the shed is shadowy and smells of sawdust. Classical piano floats from a radio. A ship's deck rises from the sunken floor like a half-buried remnant of the Great Flood. Out of the gloom walks a six-foot man with sun-burned skin, Nordic features and close-cropped grey-blond hair.

Ed Lawrence looks around fifty in his faded sweatshirt, navy sweatpants and worn workboots. Born in Maine, he saw Bay St. Lawrence for the first time in 1973, was taken with it and decided to make it home. He does not seem overly surprised to find a car full of strangers at his door. When I say I hear he's building a boat he half-smiles. "I've spent my life as a commercial fisherman," he allows, "but I've always wanted a sailing vessel."

Well, not just any sailing vessel. He wanted one with the big blocks, ropes and other trappings of the old-style fishing heritage he so loved. He wanted a boat that was seaworthy enough to fight through the North Atlantic breakers but compact enough to find shelter in the shallowest harbour. At a certain point, he just had to admit to himself, he wanted Slocum's *Spray*. I'm mesmerized as he explains how he located and bought Slocum's original plans. And then how he hired a Chéticamp boat builder to make the hull. For the past eleven years Lawrence has been doing the rest of the work himself, on nights and weekends, or days like today when he was out in his lobster boat at 3 a.m. but came in early because of a gale.

"Right on schedule," he says, fondling the detailed woodwork and gleaming bronze. He recites the dimensions like some kind of liturgy: 37 feet on deck, 14 feet 2 inches at the beam, a 5-foot draft. When I ask about the name, *Double Crow,* Lawrence repeats an old rhyme: "One crow sorrow, two crows joy." When I inquire how much money he's sunk into her, Lawrence stops to think for a minute, as if he's never considered the question before in his life.

"Well, let's see ... I must have $100,000 in it, I guess."

As he says this his wife, Margrit, appears in the doorway. She wears a bulky sweater against the cold. She is another nomad: Swiss-born, Ontario-raised, she was on a trip across Canada when she met Lawrence and his obsession. "I just wish he'd finish it," she says. "Has he told you this has been going on for eleven years?"

She laughs, but in a way that makes me think I'm edging into somewhere I shouldn't. I ask if I can use the washroom. Once inside the house I'm reluctant to leave. The scattered toys, the immaculate plank floors, the cast-iron woodstove, the piano with the open songbook, the view of the crashing ocean and this wild, elemental place—right now this just seems like the warmest, safest spot on the face of the earth. Back in the shed I take a couple of snaps while Lawrence shows Belle around the workshop. Then I persuade him to pose outside by his lobster traps. It's blowing something fierce now. When I say as much Lawrence replies, "Oh, it gets a lot worse than this. We still have boats out there today." We both look oceanwards. Even if lobster is going for six dollars a pound, the thought of being on a dickey little boat with only a few inches of wood separating me from the waves is just too much. My face goes slack with reverence. Lawrence says something lost in the winds. I ask him to repeat it. He bends closer and says, "I tell people that this isn't the end of the world. It is the beginning."

I suppose it is possible: Slocum could have ended up here, blown by some particularly long and brutal winds nearly a century ago. Then decided to live out the rest of his life anonymously rather than spoil the perfect ending to his myth. At the very least his spirit endures. So does his brazen brand of confidence. You need that kind of self-assurance when you're doing something the rest of the world—even your own wife—thinks is plain nuts. I see it all the time in Nova Scotia, where, let's face it, just living here can seem like a demented act of faith to some people. Even growing up I understood I was amongst people who dreamt big, strange dreams. Then I met Gregg Ernst and realized that even within this obsessed bunch there were some who loomed over the rest.

Ernst packs 315 pounds on his five-eleven frame. He's got a 22-inch neck, a 57-inch chest, and his biceps are 21 inches around. He is also a really nice guy—a hard-working father, husband and pillar of his local Pentecostal church. "I guess I'm sort of a traditionalist," he once told me in a gentle voice that, once you knew a little more about him, seemed as incongruous as Mike Tyson's little-boy lisp. "I like to lift things you could imagine the strongmen of ancient Greece lifting." So he hoists cars and teams of oxen, hauls eighteen-wheelers down the highway, tosses six-hundred-pound boulders around like balsa wood. If you ask him what the big rock in his basement is for, he'll drop down to the floor, clutch it to his chest and start effortlessly pounding off situps. He just cannot help himself. Because what Ernst has wanted to do at least since the age of twelve, when he lifted a ton of sheet metal off the ground, is to be the strongest man who ever lived.

I first read about him in a newspaper story about how he stole the show at a Symphony Nova Scotia fundraiser by loading two grand pianos and eighteen people on a six-hundred-pound elevated wooden platform and then raising the whole thing an inch or so off the ground. There's a mule-like quality to the back lift, Ernst's specialty. A couple of years earlier he piled 5,340 pounds onto his platform, stepped into the cutaway section, bent down and shouldered the whole thing. As always he heard a noise "like ropes going taut." But all the muscles, bones and ligaments stayed intact long enough for him to raise the load for a second. Since then he's had this ongoing battle with the *Guinness Book of Records* about whether that was the most weight anyone has hoisted unassisted. A century ago, guys like his idol Louis Cyr, the Montreal policeman who could heft more than five hundred pounds with one finger, were real heroes. But these are hard times for strongmen. He scrapes out a meagre existence for his wife and their six children by working their 280 acres of farmland and putting on the occasional exhibition of strength. It makes me kind of sad to see him on a television ad for a bar called Curly Portables, chomping on a burger and warning viewers, "Don't make me come and get you." But a man has to make a living. And Ernst needs his groceries: a couple of pounds of red meat and a gallon of yogurt, loads of oats—uncooked with apple juice and raisins—and huge servings of South Shore sauerkraut each day.

Sometimes I think about him training in that dark cellar that reminds me of a torture chamber, loading more and more weight onto that rack of his, hoping the body will hold up one more time. Chasing some long-dead ghost in the record books. And I think: How does he do it? *Why* does he do it? Which is just the sort of attitude that explains why people like me are simply not meant for greatness and others are.

Like Howard Dill, a skinny, red-haired guy in his sixties, with rheumy eyes and a chain smoker's rasp. He looks for all the world as if he just walked out of a 1930s prairie dust storm. Not at all like the man who, as his biography, *The Pumpkin King,* points out, ranks as "the Babe Ruth of pumpkin growers, the Sultan of Squash, the king of Cucurbits."

I had better admit it here and now: I once had a slight prejudice against Dill, the result of three years at a newspaper that ran one too many pictures of him posing with one of his award-winning vegetables, gourds or whatever it is pumpkins are. So it is perversely pleasant to finally meet him in person on his Windsor farm and discover he has become a prisoner of the weirdest kind of fame. "Oh, it never ends for me," he explains inside his office. "The interviews, the newspapers, the television stations, the bus tours. The whole thing started out on a local competitive level. But little did I know what God had in store for me. That I'd win all those world championships and have this big worldwide seed business. Yes, God's hand works in mysterious ways."

No "aw, shucks, it was nothing" here. Dill has an ego the size of one of his pumpkins. This is a man, after all, who also claims that the first-ever game of hockey was played on a pond on his 250-acre property back in the 1800s. Then adds, "Who in the heck cares in Japan where the game of hockey was created? But there are thousands of people over there growing Howard Dill's Atlantic giants." He has a point. Moreover, he has passion. It may be for pumpkins, but I can forgive a person almost anything if they have passion. I find my preconceptions melting away. I listen intently as he brags about all the pumpkin-growing championships he's won and all the half-assed celebrities who have taken up the hobby in recent years: Eddie Albert, members of the Texas Hunt family, Raymond Burr, even Earl Morrall, the old Baltimore Colts quarterback.

I am still paying attention as he explains how, with his grade nine education, he learned enough about genetics to breed these monsters. He takes me through the actual growing process while we wander across his dairy and fruit farm towards the pumpkin patch. It is still early in the growing season and the pumpkins are not much bigger than the ones I am used to at the Halifax farmer's market. But he's always hoping that another champion will erupt from the soil. "You've got to remember that when I broke the eight-hundred-pound mark it was like breaking the four-minute mile," he says. When he finally sends me packing I leave with a pile of his press clippings and his biography. In my pocket there are also a couple of packets of Atlantic Giant seeds, the same variety that generates a couple of million a year in sales from Dill wannabes around the world.

My route takes me back through Windsor, and I find myself driving by the home of Thomas Chandler Haliburton, the town's other famous son. He was a rural judge, politician and polemicist who hit it big by creating a Yankee peddlar named Sam Slick and writing about his travels through Nova Scotia. Haliburton was the first Canadian writer of international stature; in his heyday he rivalled Dickens in popularity over in London, where he eventually bought a mansion on the Thames. But lately, back in North America his reputation has been taking a beating, sparked by an upcoming biography that found Slick's creator to be a vicious, mean-spirited, racist, misogynist right-winger. Such, I guess, is the ephemeral nature of fame. The thing is, Haliburton just wrote books. Howard Dill is the father of the Atlantic Giant. Which is another matter altogether. He has immortality in him.

■   ■   ■

Weymouth, which sits a bit inland from the Bay of Fundy, is an elu-
sive place, veiled in green and hidden by hills. From the hills flows
the Sissiboo River, which, legend has it, got its name when a shaggy
coureur de bois pointed out half a dozen owls roosting nearby and
exclaimed, "Regardez! Six hiboux" or something like that. I immediately get the sense that a fresh start would be difficult here: Loyalist
settlement, shipping centre, lumbering village, just driving through
the town makes it clear that Weymouth's successive pasts are ineradicable and inescapable. I had never heard of the spot until, while
attending a Liberal Party convention in Halifax, I was introduced to
a delightful, sturdy-looking Grit in his early fifties named Desire, or
Desi, Belliveau. Right off he struck me as a straight-ahead, positive
kind of guy. No surprise to hear he served as the party's chief orga-
nizer in fiercely Liberal Digby County, as well as Weymouth's de facto
director of industrial development. We talked for a couple of minutes
and he said: "You come up and see me. We'll go back in the woods,
we'll cook some steaks and I'll show you Electric City."

When I arrived he was where he promised to be: running his
Foodland franchise on Weymouth's main drag. Today, it turns out,
he is a little pressed for time. Instead of steaks he fills a Styrofoam
cooler with sandwiches, cheese, pop and juice, ties up some loose
ends in the store and leads me out into the parking lot to his half-
ton. We are headed back seventeen miles into the woods. First, we
have to stop and get a guide, Lionel Borden, district superintendent
of the local pulp mill. We climb into a heavy-duty truck, painted

green and white, the company logo on the side. With Borden behind the wheel we move from pavement to dirt road. At times, a strip of grass brushes against the undercarriage. At times we are on no road at all, just thumping across exposed boulders and through streams, the branches bouncing off our roof in a mad conga rhythm. We stop to see a weird glacial formation known as the Balancing Rock, then we just keep on going.

What was he thinking? What was going through Emile Stehelin Sr.'s mind when he came way back here a century ago to build his city of light? I can accept that the Alsatian-born businessman who got rich off a felt factory in Normandy wanted to put as much distance as possible between his draft-aged sons and the shadows of war in Europe. And that the Eudists, a hard-line French religious order building a college in Nova Scotia, at Church Point, were maybe just the ones to straighten his boys out. But all I can conclude is that he must have secretly relished the thought of seeing Jean Jacques, his dissolute older son, getting off the train at Church Point that sunny, warm July day in 1892. He wore a stylish Parisian-cut grey checked suit, shiny black dress ankle boots buttoned down the sides, a melon-shaped Edwardian dark grey hat and a high-collared pinkish shirt with wide necktie neatly held in place by a good stick pin. I wish I was there to see the faces of the dirty unshaven woodsmen and fishermen when this vision stepped out of the train. A family history written by a nephew said that they tipped their hats and smiled deferentially. I don't believe it for a second. I see them knocking his hat off, spitting tobacco juice on his shirt front, then shoving him into the mud to see if he cried.

When Borden finally stops the car it is alongside a clear, lively stream. We walk past some white spruce and sugar maples towards a lake. Belliveau points to an area of scrub trees and low grass. "Now, Lionel, this is where the sawmill was, wasn't it." Except for our voices it is absolutely quiet. Nothing at all like the way it must have sounded and looked thirty years before electricity came to the rest of the area, when the Stehelin mill was running full out, when the locomotive *Maria Thérèse* was puffing along the tracks of the family-owned Weymouth and New France Railway, hauling Stehelin lumber all the way to the wharfs of Weymouth. When light poured from every building on the property and from the reflectors mounted on poles around the square. By then the whole clan was living in New France, which is what they called the family compound.

We walk over to the ruin of the main house, once home to the parents, the children and their offspring. We pass the site of the old cookhouse, where the workmen ate their hardy lumber-camp meals, then after a day in the woods passed the night dancing to the fiddle, mouth organ and jew's harp. The office with the little glass wicket where they lined up on Saturday night for their week's pay once stood over there. Near the spot where the hung-over, guilt-wracked men worshipped in Our Lady of the Forest Chapel the following morning. Desi points out the mossy rocks and the huge mushrooms growing in the remains of a stone wine cellar. After we walk a little farther, he gestures towards the sandy beach where the casino stood and, his voice low with reverence, says, "It must have been *really* something, wasn't it."

The patriarch usually wore a fine waxed moustache, corduroy suits, a long coat and high, stiff collar. He was a bit of a brooder who could kill an afternoon anguishing over the big, unsolvable metaphysical questions. But he also received fall hunters and visitors from the European nobility at his home and won the nickname of the Old Gentleman for the fair way he treated his workers. Emile Sr. watched his children marry and leave the compound in search of their own lives. Everyone who left New France took some of its laughter and spirit with them. The nights grew longer and quieter for the parents, the house bigger. When the matriarch, Marie Thérèse, died, Emile couldn't stand living there alone. One day he released a flock of white pigeons in the loft at the top of the barn, rode his old mount, Faithful, for the last time and rented a house in Weymouth.

In town Emile held on to his old ways—the French cuisine served by his black servant, good wine, long dinners followed by quiet time in the salon over coffee, liqueurs and books. The calm was broken by the declaration of World War One and the threat of military service from which Emile had tried so hard to shield his sons. Five of them were called up by the French government. The day the last of them left, the old gentleman gathered them close and gave each his fatherly blessing with a cross on each forehead and a kiss on each cheek, along with the words, "God be with you. You know where your duty lies, be sure you fulfil it well." Then he wended his way back home on the arm of Louis, the only son still at his side. He kept an up-to-date map of the European hostilities on his wall and every day walked with dog and cane down to the Western Union Telegraph office, where news from the front was posted in the window. He died on August 8, 1918, not knowing who won the war and whether his sons had survived.

They came back alive, but not necessarily to Weymouth. Six of them returned to Europe to live on the old family land. The ones who stayed behind in Nova Scotia tried to keep the property in the family, but eventually it was sold, changed hands a couple of times, then was bought by the billionaire Irving family of New Brunswick.

Strolling back to the truck, Borden points out a few of the old apple trees and the new-growth forest that has grown up around the last remaining signs of the Electric City. It's so quiet, I say dreamily. "There are no birds," he points out. "The DDT killed all the birds. Only the bugs survived." Not long after the Stehelins left, the forest inched towards the square, cutting off the view of the lakes and the casino beach. Vandals stripped the place. Ghosts naturally took up residence—phantom trains, chain rattlers, a fiery rider on a fierce black horse who unsheathed his sword before disappearing into the old wine cellar.

It feels strange to be here, at the site of this magnificent failure that went the way of so many of the bizarre, grandiose schemes hatched in this province. I like the panache and vaingloriousness of it, the mythic quality of the whole enterprise. The trail seems longer and tougher going out. At one point we stop, pull off the road and have our lunch. Then we are back at the parking lot and civilization, saying goodbye to Borden and sliding into Belliveau's truck. He wants to give me a quick tour of the area before he gets back to work. As we drive he tells me about the thickness of the fog on St. Marys Bay and the cold water "no good for anything except lobster." He tells me about Digby County politics and what makes a good rappie pie and the vagaries of the grocery store business. He explains that Weymouth, with its Loyalist beginnings, is mostly English, making it a bit of an aberration on the French shore of the province. It also has a black community, small and dirt-poor like many of the rural pockets throughout the province. He points to a tiny structure off the road. "See that yellow house, the bungalow? That's where Sam Langford was supposedly born."

Now there's a familiar name. Langford started his boxing career in Boston as a lightweight, then moved up to welterweight, middleweight and light heavyweight before finishing as a heavyweight. Here's how the Marquis of Queensbury, son of boxing's patron, described him: "Excepting only [Jack] Johnson, no heavyweight in the world could have stood up against the Boston Tar Baby in a finish fight. A freak was this amazing negro—fourteen stone of whipcord muscle and bone under a jet black skin—a neck as big as another man's thigh, a chest like a barrel, arms so grotesquely long he could scratch his ankles without stooping—and he stood five-foot-four in his bare feet. But it was his reach—84 inches—that made him the devastating fighter that he unquestionably was; in a word—a human gorilla." Georges Carpentier, the light heavyweight champion of the world, dodged him. Middleweight champ Stanley Ketchel ducked him. Same went for the great Jack Johnson, who outweighed the Nova Scotian by thirty-five pounds and whomped him something awful when they met near the turn of the century, but was still worried enough not to sign for a rematch. Consequently, Langford had to settle for a bunch of lesser titles, the Welsh middleweight crown and the heavyweight championships of England, Spain and Mexico, winning the last one despite being legally blind at the time.

But I remember him more from an old black-and-white photo. It was taken in a New York ghetto rooming house where an enterprising reporter found him alone, penniless and almost blind. His once magnificent, now ruined body was covered in a mouldy bathrobe as he sat wearing dark glasses in a rocking chair. I was just a kid when I saw the photograph. But it haunts me still. Big dreams, I suppose I realized even then, do not necessarily end in triumph. Not by a long shot. Which is why it is such a sublime surprise when the unexpected does happen.

'Folk Art,' reads the hand-painted sign near Camperdown, sending me inland through forest, past farmland until it's the end of a dead-end road. The car door slams, then nothing but sweet country silence. In a studio smelling of wood chips and paint, a brightly coloured yard-high stick fisherman, eyeballs bulging a foot out of his head, stares at me. "This is the scallop shucker here," explains its creator, Ransford Naugler. "He reached down to shuck the scallop and he flipped up the top to look in and the scallop shocked the scallop shucker, because the scallop already had his boots on."

My friend Dan Callis likes taking photographs, angling for salmon, playing the congas and smoking cigars. He also likes folk art—not the awful cutesy stuff but the real thing. He says the Naugler brothers are it: collectors from California to Israel own their stuff; gallery owners from New York leave with their van shocks sagging under the full load. I'm no judge. But these guys do have eyes. Of that I feel sure, walking past the country-western combo made up entirely of bears, the lion tamer with the lion chewing on his leg, the strange shapes and colours and designs. I feel as if I've drunk too much coffee.

Ransford, who has a round face covered with a day's growth and wears jeans, workboots and a blue workshirt over his thick trunk, only adds to the hallucinogenic mood as he explains his transformation into folk art giant. "I was a fisherman, working on the trawlers, and when I was laid off the boats I needed something else to do. I'd go do maintenance work, or I'd be a carpenter's helper, or do construction work, or anything to make it go," he says. "I was always fooling around carving and such and making homemade skis and taking old trees that fall and carving them down. But I didn't know anything about folk art back then. The first two pieces I made were a beaver and an eagle. I made a few more things and, *Jesus,* I showed them to a few guys and they said, 'Gee whiz, that's folk art.' So I called Christ Huttington and he came and had a look and he said, 'Oh, yes, that's folk art.' So he suggested I take it to Alma Houston and she said, 'Oh, yes, it's folk art, all right.' That was 1988, and that's how I got started."

We walk around some more and look at his stuff.

"What is folk art, anyway?" I finally ask.

"It's something that comes right out of your head," he replies without hesitation. "And you make it as you think it should be, not what somebody else says. If it doesn't suit me, then I can keep doing it until it does suit me. I just dream it up. It comes right out of my brain. I just visualize it."

Now that is as good a common-sense explanation of the creative process as I have ever heard. I take his card, a chunk of cardboard with his name on it, and head out into the sunlight. Next door, by a sign that says 'Leo's Art,' stands a lean, friendly-faced man with big sideburns and a worn cap adorned with a tractor logo. A few seconds later, Leo, Ransford's younger brother, is smiling sheepishly and confiding to me with wonder, "You know they call me an artist." Then we are inside his cool, dark little shed looking at his work, which to my untrained eye is every bit as whimsical and wild as his brother's. "Oh, Ransford, he started about three months before I did," he explains quietly. "I started January 13, 1989, in the afternoon. And Bradford Naugler, down in Middlewood, he started about two weeks after I did. We all just learned ourselves, I guess, as we went along. Even my dad. I used to visit him quite often and liked what he was doing. He was the guy who nagged me to do folk art. I told him, 'No, I couldn't do folk art.' But one day, when there was nobody around, I thought I'd make a goose, and nobody was going to see it. Well, it turned out pretty good, and a fella called Christ Huttington come along and he bought it."

There seem to be a lot of Nauglers creating folk art, I say.

"Me and my two brothers, and my brother-in-law, James Swiggey. He's in the hospital right now; he had a bad attack of kidney stones. He wanted to go to the Lunenburg Folk Festival, but it don't look too good. If he can't blast the big kidney stones out in Bridgewater today, they'll have to send him to Halifax. And then, well, Adam Wade, my nephew, is doing it. And Craig Docker down in Middlewood—he's my brother's son—he's doing it. And Bradford's wife, well, she claims she ain't doing it, but she's been painting now for the last year. And my mother, she does painting too. Yes, it's good fun."

He shows me some of the work for the upcoming Lunenburg festival—a fowl with a split personality who doesn't know if it is a hen or a goose, a flying elephant, a series of indescribably strange and colourful chairs, love seats and tables. "I used to do auto body work. Yeah, I got a body shop right down there—that's where my nephew works now—and I was doing that for thirteen years. You go back into Mahone Bay a ways and the Holy Mackerel Gallery has got one of my metal pieces there. It's got a cast-iron sink on the bottom of it, then two disc brake pads off a 1980 Dodge Omni for the feet, and hollow pieces of pipe for legs. The body is a propane tank of a travel trailer, and the tail feathers are the springs off a Cherokee Jeep. The wings are the bumper off a Chev truck and the neck and the head was off of a 750 Honda motorcycle exhaust. Then I made bells for on to it, and I called it Bella the Swan. There's a lot of fun into them. But I make them the way I want to make them, and if somebody tries to tell me how to make them, I always tell them no, I make them my own way."

Outside I should be savouring the silence, the sun on my face and the earthy smell of a wood fire somewhere, but I am too busy wondering about human nature. How a little artistic freedom might mean as much to one man as a feat of strength large enough for the ages does to another. They are all big dreams, born in the soul and forged in the heart.

Ten

Pilgrims and Shrines

—

THE MORNING AFTER THE ONLY NIGHT I EVER SPENT IN THE TOWN OF Parrsboro I awoke to find my nostrils swollen shut from twelve hours of inhaling forest-fire smoke blown down across the Bay of Fundy from New Brunswick. I staggered to my feet, made it to the bathroom, then sneezed forty-seven times in rapid succession before swallowing a Sinutab. I was beginning to feel marginally human again by the time I entered the dining room at the nice inn where I was staying. Coffee, or maybe half a dozen cups, and I'll be almost indistinguishable from the other upright walkers. I spy the life-giving pot on the buffet table, load up with food while I'm there and head for a window seat. My path takes me past two middle-aged, bald, bespectacled men sitting silently together. I saw them last night, wandering arm in arm the way European men sometimes do, along the harbour.

Antisocial as I feel, greetings are unavoidable. "Dib u gum for the blay?" I sputter, assuming they were here for last night's perfor-mance at the local theatre.

The shorter, huskier version grins, turns his back towards me and says, "That's why we're here." His navy blue T-shirt is emblazoned with:

1945

World War II ends

United Nations is established

the microwave oven is invented

George Orwell's Animal Farm is written

Anne Murray is Born

"My name is Horst," he says, spinning back around and sticking out a stubby paw. "This is my twin brother, Peter, who is five minutes younger. We are Anne Murray's greatest Austrian fans."

I just stand there, eyes streaming, mouth open trying to swallow air, fighting through the fog to try to assimilate this new information. Not knowing really what to do, I shake hands with Peter, who is a little taller and thinner. He flashes me a sad grin. Horst, who it turns out is fifty-four and teaches English literature and German at a Viennese high school, pushes out a chair and invites me to join them. Now who, no matter how bad they felt, could turn down such an invitation? Soon as I sit down he seizes my shoulder and begins a staccato, rapid-fire monologue.

"I learned English listening to the songs of Elvis Presley and Pat Boone. Then I found out about Anne. She helps me to be strong. When she sings 'Some days are good and some days are bad/some days it rains, some days it shines' it helps you to help yourself. Next to sports—jogging and swimming—she is where I turn to solve my problems. I have a framed picture of her in the middle of my living room. I have all of her CDs. Listening to her music I feel in harmony with myself and the world. Do you know she has a cottage near here? I went to see her and told her husband that I am in love with your wife."

I weigh this information carefully, knowing that the Songbird from Springhill has spent the last decade or so with a crazed Saskatchewan wheat farmer stalking her. Peter, who kept eating throughout his brother's breathless delivery, excuses himself. Once he's beyond earshot Horst leans forward and confides, "I have got problems with my twin brother who is manic depressive and is always trying to commit suicide. My whole life has been spent looking after him. It is hard, but I don't complain. I have studied Shakespeare and all the German philosophers. But if I need help I just need to listen to Anne and I will know that she will help me and save me. Anne makes me stay strong, positive and optimistic about life. I am indebted to her for helping me get through my days."

A lot to handle first thing in the a.m. Even if Horst isn't babbling strangely, he's got far too much spark for me at this hour. I keep waiting for the caffeine to mercifully kick in. But nothing happens. I slump lower and lower in my chair. Peter returns. Some small talk, then they're getting up. I walk them to the parking lot.

"A picture?" I inquire, holding up my camera.

"Why not," says Horst, chuckling. It takes a few seconds to get them in place. Then I snap—Horst, on the passenger's side, beaming like a man with purpose, Peter on the driver's seat, right hand raised in farewell, smiling his melancholy smile.

Lumbering, blueberries, shipbuilding and the amazing Fundy tides used to keep this area alive. Now this is the Land Time Forgot. Water fades in and out of sight as the road from Parrsboro twists and bucks, climbs and plummets. Only a short drive to Advocate Harbour, where a hundred vessels once rolled from the slips each year. Now it's a ghost town, with a big wild west sky and a cemetery on the hill with a number of headstones bearing the brief epitaph "Lost at Sea." It is one of the more desolate places I've seen in the province.

On the outskirts of Springhill a well-dressed guy in the doorway of a car dealership gives me directions. Thirty seconds later I'm lost again, driving back and forth along the same street like a beat cop. I stop and ask a pair of skinny lads with rattail haircuts how to get to the Miners' Museum. Speaking loudly and very slowly, as if to a child or a foreigner, one of them takes all of 20 seconds to lay out the simple route. "Jeez, there's lots of signs, buddy," I hear his companion mumble as I roll up the window. "This isn't New York friggin' City."

No, it isn't. Just your everyday mining town, once the last shift punches out. Stan Pashkoski is on duty at the museum. He's sixty-seven, with a broad, happy Slavic face. He looks like he sleeps in the miner's overalls. There are twelve of us, sporting identical helmets, rubber boots and yellow rubber rain jackets. I catch my reflection in a window: I look like a canary-coloured Pez dispenser.

We follow him on a 45-degree angle down into the mine shaft. It's damp, warm and claustrophobic. Hell of a way to make a living. Or to die. He tells us about the 1891 disaster, which claimed 125 lives, the subterranean fire in 1916, and the 1956 explosion, which killed thirty-nine men and captured the attention of the world as reporters broadcast live from the site waiting for news of survivors. He tells us about the "bump" of 1958, which claimed seventy-five. He turns off the underground lights to give us a sense of what it is like to be buried underground. We just stand there in the dark not saying a word.

When we're back above ground Stan tells me he started working in the mines at sixteen. "It was a way of life, the only thing you knew how to do, and the money was not bad at the time. In 1956 I was a supervisor and had come out of the mine a half-hour before the explosion. Of course, I was immediately called to be on the rescue crew. In 1958, I was above ground when the bump took place. I was due to go to work at 11 p.m. and the bump came at seven. Again I was on the rescue crew. I quit after that, when they closed the mine."

The end of coal mining just about killed the town, he said. Then in 1975 a fire that started in a small restaurant gutted the downtown. He shows me a newspaper story listing the casualties: Nelson's Book Store, the Knights of Pythias Building with its laundromat and Brown's Flower Shop, Letcher's Building, Capital Theatre, John Smith's Mens Wear, the Cookie Box pastry shop, the T. Eaton order office, town hall and the police station, Mrs. Knight's home, McLean's Shoe Store, Casey's Burger Shop, James Demetre's Candy Kitchen, Letcher's Furniture Store, the Springhill *Record* office, the Halifax *Herald* office, Ryan's Storage building. "A lot of those buildings are still unoccupied," he says with a shrug of his big shoulders. "Not much industry here. Tourism is the future. But it's a tough town. Always survived."

Yes, it still has hopes. Springhill isn't a pretty town, not by a long shot. But it has Anne Murray and the Anne Murray Centre, and maybe that's all a place that wants to dream really needs. The first bars of "Snowbird" float from inside the building as I approach; a middle-aged woman in a pinkish uniform hovers at the entrance. "Not really," she laughs when I ask if she gets sick of listening to the same songs over and over again. "She made so many we can switch the tapes." A tour bus from Vermont has just pulled into the parking lot and the seniors begin to step out. "Museum or washroom?" she asks with a smile as the first one comes carefully up the stairs.

There is Anne Murray's newborn outfit, her report cards, including one that said "Morna Ann Murray highest marks grade VI"; her vaccination certificate, October 11, 1950, made out by her father, J.C. Murray, M.D. There is a life-saving course certification, a photo of a sixteenth birthday sleepover, another of her barefoot on the *Singalong Jubilee* TV show, her graduation program (phys ed) from the University of New Brunswick, mementoes of Anne Murray Day in Toronto, of appearing in the Rose Bowl Parade and being made honorary deputy mayor of Moose Jaw. Her gowns—

the sparkly one from the Roy Thomson Hall performance, the one from the Australia tour, the one she wore during her last National Arts Centre appearance in Ottawa—glitter inside a glass case. There are videos of her performing love duets with k.d. lang and television specials with Glen Campbell. There are pictures of her and Richard Hatfield, Armand Assante, Annette Funicello, Ruth Buzzi, Frank Gorshin, Johnny Cash, Dionne Warwick, Alan Thicke and Dennis Weaver.

I feel the senior citizens gaining on me, loud as soccer hooligans, so I start for the parking lot, then, on a whim, stop to look at the guest book. Under yesterday's heading in lovely handwriting that takes up twice the normal amount of space is written:

> Anne, you make my life worth living, maybe I'll see you
>   (together with my wife Irene) some day,
> Love,
> Horst from Vienna
> I'd like to swim with you across the ocean! Horst
>   I'll be your eyes, my candle & you show me the way—
> Thanks, Anne!

Now, there's a lot of hocus-pocus concerning Nova Scotia. For a variety of reasons the province has emerged as a kind of New Age beacon. Harmonic convergences, energy vortexes, power centres, alien sightings, renegade gurus, goofy religious movements, Nova Scotia has got them all. At times it can seem as though everyone is some kind of obsessive, a weird pilgrim here in search of some freaky shrine. I used to run into them and wonder: why? Until something dawned that was so obvious that to utter it in public meant the risk of being handed a cap and bells: we are all gone in our own way, the searcher for contentment and connection as much as the guy atop the hill trying to channel back to a former life. So why not?

I love driving aimlessly. Travelling is more fun—hell, life is more fun—if you can treat it as a series of impulses. So I like to stop when something catches my eye. That happens all the time. I am, for instance, driving through the fog up along the west coast of Cape Breton when Belle, who is four at the time, points and yells, "Dad, Dad, Dad! Looook!" On a nice day, I'm sure Joe's Scarecrows are a glorious scene. But today, the dozens of store mannequins in rubber masks and costumes set in a semicircle in this open field just look forlorn, even a little scary, like a kids' playground designed by Michael Jackson. We get out anyway and walk around. I circle warily by Pierre Trudeau in army fatigues and René Lévesque, a smoke dangling from his lip. I narrowly miss knocking over an old crone in a wedding dress, then, turning, almost take off the wrinkled headset adorning a checked man's suit with a note pinned to it saying: "Well, well, well, you finally made it to visit us. For the love of God shake on it I'm Duncan."

One day I am passing through Maitland, another long-ago ship-building centre, which sits at the elbow of the Bay of Fundy a little southwest of Parrsboro. I stop into the tourist bureau where a conservatively dressed woman looks up from her desk and says, "What the hell do you want?" Actually she said, "Can I help you?" but with such a note of surprise that an actual tourist must have been the last thing she expected to see walk through that door. I gathered up some bumf and took it out to the car, where I read that in 1831, before the big shipbuilding boom that put the place on the map, there were eleven shingled houses in Maitland, four of which were taverns. Maitland still has a well-preserved store, an old Norman Rockwell barber shop and a vintage courthouse, as well as a startling number of ornate, preserved-in-aspic homes. The literature identifies the houses as "gems of Greek Revival, soaring Gothic Revival, Second Empire, Classical Revival (Cape Cod) or Classical Revival (Colonial) styles."

Down the highway a couple of hundred yards is a sign that says Springhurst. I park in the small lane and look the place up in my literature. The home, I learn, was built by Harris Neil, a local builder. It's designed in a Victorian Gothic style "with a front facade that features a two-storey central bay flanked by ground-floor bay windows and bracketed gables over the second-floor windows." I had been forewarned that Roy Rhyno, the village amateur historian who lives here, sometimes likes to greet people at the door in eighteenth-century costume. But today the small man with the glasses sports a pair of shorts, tube socks, sneakers and a white and green T-shirt advertising the Maitland Heritage Festival. He's slightly bowlegged, but sturdy, the type of resolute soul you'd run into on some isolated hiking trail cheerfully whistling the strains of "Colonel Bogey" as he chugs along. A man, it quickly becomes apparent, with enthusiasms. "I used to teach history at one of the local schools," he explains as he ushers me into the low-ceilinged original kitchen. "That and architecture are what interest me."

He leads me into a couple of dimly lit antiquey rooms, then through a doorway as he says humbly, "I thought we could talk in here." I bet he relishes these moments: the occasion when someone new walks into the room for the first time, takes one look and fractures their chin on the floor. The thirty-foot ceilings and glistening marble floors, the exotic Asian sculptures, vases and paintings, the huge, lush plants—the likes of which I've never seen—the rich, ornate ship's scroll-work hanging high on the wall. I turn, half-expecting to see Rhyno now wearing harem slippers and puffing on a hookah like some Victorian adventurer as he begins to recount his experiences in the flesh pots of Cairo. Instead, he just stuffs some tobacco in his pipe. Then begins telling me about Maitland.

A shipbuilder named Alfred Putnam once owned Springhurst. Rhyno's chest puffs with pride as he takes me around the rest of the house and explains all the effort he's gone to keeping it in its original shape. I nod enthusiastically, saying, "Uh-huh, uh-huh, uh-huh ... I see ... Really ... Wow," as we move from room to room. There's a caught-in-a-time-warp quality to the monarchy memorabilia, the antiques, the minutely detailed ship's models and the huge collection of ceramic Lorenz mushrooms. But it's the mannequins I can't take my eyes off—big as life, and dressed in formal costume from some long-gone era. They stand nonchalantly, inclined in a variety of life-like poses in each successive room we enter. If the light came in a little differently you'd swear they could move. Then a robed figure with long, wispy hair seated facing the window does: just a small twitch of the neck and shoulders, but it is enough to send memories of every bad *Psycho* knockoff I've ever seen flooding back to me. Rhyno doesn't register my alarm. "Sorry to be rushing you out the door," he says, "but we're having people for lunch."

In spots there is an otherworldly aspect to the province—no surprise for a place to which people are drawn for some truly strange reasons. Tom Haynes-Paton has a long, white pony-tail, a gentle face, calm voice and the perfect demeanour for someone who spent twenty-five years as a missionary in Japan. Now he lives outside the scallop-fishing centre of Digby, where he runs an oriental art gallery and an immersion centre for businesspeople, diplomats and anyone else who wants a quick indoctrination into all things Japanese. Ask how he came to be on the lip of the Bay of Fundy in a freshly painted wooden house around which flute music and bright-coloured banners flicker and he has a tendency to say things like: "Because I just want to quiet the mind, achieve inner peace and manifest peace and love at a very deep level. I worked as a missionary, in the civil rights movement and human rights and community organizing. We chose to try to change the hearts of people, which is the only way to change government. But then after a long time in one of the world's largest cities—and finally for love and love of the land—I chose to come here and live because I wanted a life of peaceful contemplation, and I felt Nova Scotia was the most peaceful spot in the world."

He means peace in the incense burning, sitting in the lotus position with the Monks of Santo Domingo De Silos on the CD player sense of the word. Talk like this normally makes me a bit nervous. But I'm listening because I am still a bit puzzled over why this odd mix of characters seem to be finding their way here. When I ask about this he nods and says, "Have you ever heard of Pangea?" Which, oddly enough, I have. Encouraged, he explains his pet theory: that it all relates back to before the geological supercontinent—Pangea—splintered apart, when Nova Scotia stood cheek-to-jowl with North Africa and the Cornwall coast of England. His feeling, if I understand correctly, is that something undefinable radiates from those rocks that Nova Scotia shares with these other mystical areas. So it's no surprise, in his view, that the dreamy Celts who roamed that other terrain would one day be drawn here. Just as it was inevitable that the Huguenots, whom he calls "the best that France had to offer," would eventually arrive. Or that the other spiritual seekers who have come since would head this way.

It is all very unexpected. The elevated chat, the Zen garden, the serene-looking Mokushi Centre—a combination home and classroom—where the students sleep on tatami mats. What does one make of this gallery, with its startling collection of Japanese woodblocks, hangings, statues and calligraphy, out here off the Trans-Canada, middle of nowhere? Or the cleared space with the carpet of grass leading out to the cliff overlooking the ocean? The long poles on each side are mounted with loudspeakers like the ones you always see in World War Two prison camp movies. Haynes-Paton explains that they carry the same early-morning Radio Taiso exercise broadcast that the nation works out to back in Japan. Then he starts to do a slow, graceful martial arts movement as I stand there looking out on the ocean.

It is a beautiful moment, and illuminating too, because it reinforces something I know but have a tendency to forget: we all see what we want. Horst sees a woman who keeps his life on track; I see miners dying. Most people see a Nova Scotia fishing cove, Haynes-Paton sees Japan. Religion is like that, same with politics, music, food and all the other great obsessions—including the thirst for home. Point-of-view is everything. Take Shelburne, which seems to me an unlikely shrine, but go figure. Last time through the mercury edged towards forty Celsius and the radio DJ kept screaming "Eeewwwwww, *it's boiling out there*" over the loud, useless rumble of the car fan. Outside there was wind, but the hot, fevered kind that brought no relief. Maybe this was the best way to see Shelburne, anyway: have it float in the mind for a while until the need for it is almost visceral. Then drive into town like into a mirage repeating "In Shelburne it will be cool," with all the desperate conviction of Hare Krishnas searching for salvation.

Once, I'm sure, it all must have sounded so promising. Back in the late nineteenth century, say, when an overenthusiastic land agent named Alexander McNutt petitioned the British crown for a charter to found a new city across the water, which he planned to call New Jerusalem. Hard to know whether that was ringing optimism, a salesman's marketing touch or maybe just a horribly twisted sense of humour. I like Shelburne's old colonial houses and buildings, the trees, the pleasant streets sloping down to the waterfront, the elliptical, rock-bound harbour. Shelburne is not hard on the eye. It's an odd, stately little place with a whiff of terminal decline about the quiet government wharf and the tarted-up bed-and-breakfasts. It looks like how Nova Scotia once must have looked. But as for ever being the face of the future—a New Jerusalem—well, I'm sorry, I just don't think so.

I'm not the first person to feel this way. The New England Loyalists, driven out of home and hearth for refusing to embrace independence and republicanism, should have known something was terribly wrong when they arrived in the mid-1700s, wandered into some cove and encountered as poor a piece of humanity as they'd probably ever laid eyes upon. Asked what in God's name he was doing here he responded with the immortal words: "Poverty brought me to Nova Scotia and poverty keeps me there." At that point there was no turning back. Port Roseway, the name the authorities had wisely chosen for the town, was the payoff for their loyalty. Soon more settlers arrived, more streets were laid out, more and more frame houses built and filled with fine furniture, silver, crystal and linen. The town grew at such an astounding pace that before long its population topped Quebec City and Montreal combined. It was for one brief moment, if you can imagine this, the fastest-growing town in the entire continent.

What happened?

It could have been disappointment over the rocky soil or the grinding ice of the winter months. Maybe they were turned off by the n'er-do-wells who crowded in brawling and wandering drunk through the streets, or the whorehouses and taverns that sprang up, giving the place a raffish, debauched air. Maybe, on the other hand, the Loyalists were simply lazy fops unaccustomed to hard labour. All anyone really knows is that before long a few people began to drift away. Then it became a flood. By 1789 two-thirds of the town was uninhabited, cattle and hogs roamed through the once-fine parlours and wine cellars. Within a decade the town's population of ten thousand had shrunk to three hundred—the great failure of the Loyalist migration was complete.

The town recovered, eventually becoming a shipbuilding centre of note before the end of the Age of Sail. Today it seems sleepy on the outskirts. But we take a couple of dickey turns in the general direction of the harbour, come around a corner, and it's as though we've driven into Martha's Vineyard on a nice summer weekend— big knots of tourists, Winnebagos, even a tour bus or two choke the streets. I remember then that an enterprising Hollywood location scout had discovered that late-twentieth-century Shelburne could be magically morphed into mid-1600s Puritan New England, and the setting for *The Scarlet Letter,* a $40-million turkey that would garner some of the harshest reviews since *Ishtar.* But I guess I had no sense of the magic of Hollywood, that people would travel long distances to see a place where Demi Moore once writhed in a grain bin, Gary Oldman sweated out last night's bender and Robert Duvall, who must have dearly needed the paycheque, skulked around in a wig and one of those Quaker tallboy hats like the world's unhappiest drag queen.

Caught up in the excitement, we want to walk down and take a look at the movie set pieces, which the town has maintained as a tourist attraction. But it is so crowded that we have to circle twice through the old Loyalist homes to find a parking spot near the small, tasteful tourist bureau. The windows are open and the room is actually cooled by a breeze off the water. It is quiet for a moment. Then a woman in a pantsuit made out of millions of shiny synthetic pink fibres pushes through the door. She mops her brow with a paper napkin, points to a photo album full of pictures from the *Scarlet Letter* film shoot and says to her husband, whom I imagine to be the Martinizing king of Poughkeepsie, N.Y., "Look, honey, there she is, Demi Moore."

Lots of people arrive in Nova Scotia with only a vague urge or idea in mind. But many know exactly what they are doing and where they are bound, no matter how strange the purpose. By summer the woods, cliffs and headlands around St. Georges Bay are covered with flowers: lupines, wild rose bushes, others I can't identify. At the Cape George Presbyterian Church at the very tip of the bay I walk among the gravestones for the old Highlanders, and see one for George Ballentine, who died on May 22, 1878, at age 81, that says, "Blessed are the dead who lie in the land." It is a pleasant enough place to be. Even when one minute the grey clouds spit rain and the next they open to splashes of sunlight, with the wind off the water filling the background like a monk's chant. Nothing frivolous about the land here. This is a place that stirs big thoughts. A place where a monk from France—his order overrun and dispersed by Napoleon's armies—might find himself in the Year of Our Lord 1825, and give a prayer of thanks.

The good Father Vincent De Paul Merle was able to persuade only a few of his brethren to return with him to lay the foundation for Petit Clairvaux, the continent's first Trappist monastery, a few miles beyond Antigonish. But that was then. By midafternoon on a Sunday 170 years later the monastery parking lot is full. I follow the crowd, most of them still dressed for church, as they pick their way along the path through the birch trees and the ferns until they come to a sign that bids visitors: *Pilgrim; Go with Jesus his cross-borne way/to Mary, our mother, her help to pray.*

From there, crosses mark the path. Among a stand of hemlock trees, we come to the shrine, a life-sized statue of Our Lady of Grace, and a spring bubbling with clean, clear water. "The discovery and blessing of the spring is credited to the third Prior of the Monastery, Father James Deportment, who came to the Monastery in 1858," a pamphlet I picked up back in the museum says. "People called it 'Holy Spring' because, as they claim, quite a few visitors were helped and a few sick 'cured' by using this water." I look behind me and am surprised—a line of supplicants snaking into the woods, their faces full of awe, devotion, and the child-like search for salvation.

Charles Gaines, who lives a few miles away, has seen those expressions before. Which is why the owner of the Petrocan station in East Tracadie grills me for a full five minutes before giving me directions to his place.

"Is that necessary?" I ask Gaines when I arrive.

"In a way, yeah," he answers. "Patricia calls them the pilgrims. They just show up here. A couple pulled in some time ago from California. They just drove up the road and said, 'We read the book and here we are.' Then we just stood there looking at each other. I mean, it's touching and humbling. It's nice to know that that little book affected people's lives in such a profound way. But I don't have any answers for people's lives. All I had to say went into that book."

That book is called *A Family Place*. It's a story of how Gaines's life in America had veered out of control, of how he almost lost everything that mattered to him. Then how he found it again here, on a piece of land in East Tracadie on St. Georges Bay, where he built a summer home and discovered that rarest of things, a second chance.

Gaines is tall and handsome. He's got a lovely wife and great kids. He hangs around with guys like Arnold Schwarzenegger (Gaines's first novel, *Stay Hungry,* was made into a movie that introduced Da Ahnold to the movie-going world) and Winston Groom, the author of *Forrest Gump,* who is coming for some fishing and shooting next week. He's always had great jobs: writing books and screenplays, running a travel business that consists of taking his rich buddies to exotic locations to hunt animals and big fish. He's rich enough to write in *A Family Place* that he bought his three hundred acres in Nova Scotia for no more than the price-tag of a Mercedes and see nothing strange about it.

We tour the property. He wears shorts and a grey T-shirt and moves well even though he had both hips replaced a couple of years back. "Life is always serving up these wonderful symbols," he says. "If running your hips into oblivion at age fifty isn't telling you that your life has gotten out of control, I don't know what is." He and Patricia moved to Ireland after university in Alabama, had kids, built a little "walled garden" that kept everything bad out. They returned in the late 1960s. His books sold well. Then came what Gaines calls the "dumb country-boy-goes-Hollywood syndrome." His next novel was a commercial and critical bust. Gaines knew that it had all come undone the moment Patricia walked into the hotel room and found him with a friend's wife in his lap blowing some kind of animal tranquillizer up his nose. She asked for a divorce; the wall had crumbled.

"We saw Nova Scotia as a refuge," he explains as we peer out at the bay, "a place where we could come and put our lives back on track, a place which still held deeply and fervently the overall ethos and the values that had disappeared from our lives. It gives Patricia and me our walled garden back. A place where we can come four or five months each year and get back in touch with each other."

We head towards the tiny, impeccably built cabin. It's only big enough for two for the precise reason that they want only the right kind of visitors—people who are willing to live in tents and won't get in the way of their work and sublimely simple lives. All of which makes "the pilgrims" a little unnerving. Even if Gaines can sort of understand why they come. "The book strikes a chord with a lot of professionally driven North American men my age who had gone through the 1980s and wound up losing touch with everything that was important to them," he explains. "I turned back the clock. They want to believe—they have to believe—that is possible."

All pilgrimages, ultimately, are private affairs done for personal reasons that make no sense to others. So maybe it is not even worth trying to explain what I was doing there standing in the middle of the highway at 5 a.m. just outside Chéticamp at the entrance to the Cabot Trail. Some weather is coming this morning. You can feel it in the air. A calm, I guess, but a forced one, as if the world is holding its breath for what is to follow. Maybe later today *les suêtes* will come screaming down from the Cape Breton Highlands National Park, churning up dust storms and sweeping the land of everything that isn't nailed down. At its worst—in winter 1993, say, when it blew the roof off the hospital—the winds can reach 150 miles an hour. Sometimes they just come roaring out of nowhere. A day like today, maybe, when the red, white and blue Acadian flags sag in the windless sky, and the clouds threaten rain.

I am dead tired. Since we don't have an alarm clock, Robert, the owner of the Parkview motel where we were staying, agreed to wake me at four-thirty. Back in the room I laid out my stuff for the morning—rod, waders, jeans, flannel shirt, an alarmingly healthy looking lunch of fig newtons, apple juice and fruit. But Belle and I have to share a bed and she wants the answers to the big questions of the universe. "Uh, Dad, um, can a cheetah run faster than Donoban Dailey? Daddy, where are we going tomorrow? Daddy, can you please stop snoring, please, Dad? Dad, what happens to a fish when you catch it? Dad, do numbers go on forever? Dad, what does God look like?"

I mumble things that make little sense even to a four-year-old. Out of desperation I fake sleep and finally actually doze off. It seems like just minutes have passed when I hear Robert spin into the parking lot, sending gravel flying. A half-moon hangs in the sky. As it brightens I can see the outline of the highlands. I hear the river, thousands of birds singing wildly somewhere, and the drone of the mosquitoes dive-bombing my head. Punchy from lack of sleep, I turn some of my lunch into breakfast, lie down on the steps of the motel office to nap, then jump up and run through some karate katas in the middle of the empty highway.

When he finally arrives, Laurie MacDonald apologizes for being late: someone had borrowed the mountain bikes we needed to make it up the long trail to the fishing holes. He's a compact thirty-year-old with long blond hair and hawkish features. Last time I saw him was on the Margaree River. Lisa and I were working one side of the river when up popped Laurie's head from some grass on the opposite bank. He waved a greeting, then silently packed his sleeping bag, pulled a canoe into the water and disappeared around the bend like the ghost of some long-ago frontiersman.

We drive a few hundred yards to the parking lot, gear up our rods and slip them into cases attached to the backs of the bicycles. The uphill path is rocky and pitted with pools of water. Laurie pulls ahead but keeps looking back as I wobble along the edge of the drop. I marvel at him. I know he doesn't mean to, but he has a knack for making people feel inadequate. Something about the way he picks his way along this lousy path, easy as if he was driving his bike through a big empty parking lot; he moves through the woods on foot the same way, never a misstep, never looking where he walks as you just try to stay upright. Adding to this perception of omnipotence is his disconcerting habit of pulling water bottles from behind rocks and hip waders out of knotholes in trees. If he stuck his hand into a log and hauled out a plate of steaming, perfectly garnished fettuccine alfredo and a nice goblet of Riesling, well, I don't think I'd be the slightest bit surprised.

We finally stop and lean the bikes against some trees, then walk through the woods until we come into a clearing. I cringe a little at the sight of the half-dozen anglers already working the river. I loathe having to fish in front of others for the simple reason that as a fly caster I make up for a lack of distance with an almost homicidal inaccuracy. I'm past the worst stage, when a really bad back cast left the line wound a couple of times around my head and body with the fly dangling limply off my nose. But casting for salmon remains more an aerobic activity for me. Flop that line out there; try to make it straight and pretty, if you can. Then do it again and again and again until you are ready to go home and get some physio. I spoke in elevated fashion about the Zen quality of the act, that kind of thing. Though secretly I was beginning to question the intelligence of spending what little free time I had standing kidney-deep in a paralyzingly cold stream.

At the root of everything was one clear problem: there are no fish. As a result, the act of fly-fishing for salmon has turned into something more than a sport. Call it a metaphysical quest, a vehicle for acquiring humility, even an exercise in gear fetishism. Bringing home a mess of salmon—that had nothing to do with it. On the Chéticamp you were not even allowed to kill them; you had to set them free. But still the anglers come, drawn to a mecca where at least you have a chance of eyeballing them.

Already present is the usual eclectic bunch: the big guy wearing the fishing hat and sunglasses is Bill, who dabbles in real estate and fishes the rest of the time while his wife makes teddy bears in the back of this trailer they drag around North America. The earth mother is Susan, a pony-tailed quilt maker from Vermont who wears a flannel plaid shirt beneath her fishing vest. The calm-looking fellow with the fourteen-foot two-handed rod is Henry, who is from Virginia, and looks far too young to be retired, but fishes here during the summers, hunts grouse in the winter and goes birding in between. The quiet guy in the park warden's outfit is Clarence, who spends each summer making his rounds on foot alone through the Cape Breton highlands. One summer, he tells me, he did 460 miles. I notice a lot of butterflies. "Those are yellow swal-lowtails," he says. He's not fishing, just talking birds with Henry for a minute before returning to his mysterious duties.

The Chéticamp, which originates in the highlands and runs right out to the ocean, is a strange little river. Might as well forget the usual fishing pattern: long casts, taking a few steps and covering the water. To raise a fish here you have to find the right lies in the rock-strewn current, and then deliver the fly from some awkward angle. "This is a test of precision," warns Laurie in what for me are truly ominous words. I try a few casts and mercifully make it through the pool without hooking someone's earlobe. I sit down and wait my turn as the others rotate in. After I run through one more time Laurie suggests we move downstream. As we do Sue manages to hook a nice twelve-pounder. Catch. Pause. Release.

Laurie climbs up on some rocks sure as a billy goat and notices something in a section of water where all I see is brown foam. "Now this is what I want you to do," he says, grabbing my rod, false casting once and laying a little parabola down some thirty feet away. Laurie is a stickler for presentation—the line has to land straight, and you've got to pull in the slack so the fly swings by on a natural arc. He smells some action now, so his commands become precise. "Put the fly over there by that rock. Okay, pull in some line. More ... more ... more. Let it swing. That's it. Okay, okay. Now right over to that rock again."

I cast again and again and again. Then I feel a tug. A fish! Now what? The chances of actually hooking one seemed so slim that I had long forgotten the suggested technique for setting the hook. I haul like a powerlifter—the classic novice's mistake—and the line pulls free. Laurie grimaces. "Okay, let's go again, the same spot." Half a dozen casts later I feel the fish again, wait a moment, pull back— and lose him again. Laurie pulls off his cap in despair, mumbles something I can only assume is some ancient Gaelic oath. I wait for him to hurl his cap to the ground and start jumping up and down on it like Yosemite Sam. Instead he lets out a long sigh, smiles at me with infinite patience and says, "John, do you think maybe this would be a good time for a break?"

Fishing guides are the most gentle folk. I have met damaged, cigar-chomping Vietnam vets, former freedom fighters in Czechoslovakia who gave up being accountants to take sports full-time, wealthy Americans who guide part of the year and paint landscapes the rest. I don't know much about Laurie, other than he went to St. F.X., played some hockey and lives on the family land on the outskirts of Chéticamp. And, of course, that he is drawn to rivers and fish. "My main goal is to stay out of cities," he says as we share a couple of ham sandwiches he pulled out of God-knows-where. "I can't live in a city. I don't have any use or need for them. I spend the rest of the year in British Columbia. I'm working on my plumbers papers. I live in a tent, just my sleeping bag, a rented car and a Coleman stove right through the winter. Usually I eat in town. That's what it takes for me to live here for four or five weeks. There they have steelhead and sea-running rain- bow trout. But I've yet to see anything like the Atlantic salmon coming up to take the fly. It is all wicked, all great."

This is what he sees: all the problems and magic of life distilled to the challenge of fooling a fish into rising to a manmade fly and then momentarily pulling it from its world into ours. That is how he finds contentment. It never comes easily.

Once, the Vidyadhara, the Venerable Chögyam Trungpa Rinpoche, a chubby, smiling guy with big ideas and intemperate habits whose heart gave out when he was in his forties, made his way through these same rolling wooden hills. He was twenty-four years out of Tibet, which he fled over the Himalayas when the Communist Chinese invaded. Not your average Cape Breton tourist: his youth was spent preparing to take charge of a series of Buddhist monasteries in Tibet. Without a country he roamed around India, England and Scotland before landing in Boulder, Colo., then blossoming as a New Age centre, where he established his loose brand of secular Buddhism. To this day his followers still cannot explain why he decided to move the worldwide headquarters for his church to Halifax in 1986. Or how he came to be up here following the same bumpy, winding road past sparse farmhouses and vacant fields beyond headlands tapering off to cliffs, beaches and green, icy waters. But he saw something here as he passed through a clump of hardwood to the spot where a series of colourful banners now flutter like a flock of birds and an oddly angled building with grey weathered shingles stands next to a small vegetable garden where three middle-aged people quietly work.

Setting up an appointment to visit Gampo Abbey, the main training and meditation centre for Trungpa Rinpoche's followers, is not
hard. Somebody at the Vajradhatu Buddhist Church in Halifax gives
you a fax number. You zip off your request. Then one day an androg-
ynous voice from a person identifying themself as T. Palmo will be
on the phone saying they would be happy to see you. "Just call
when you arrive."

T. Palmo sits behind a desk in a small, well-appointed office. She
is, I would say, two inches taller than I am. Her hair is short and
steel grey. She wears an orange tunic and a long wine-coloured
robe that reaches the floor and partially covers her big, sturdy-looking feet. She has a nice smile and a disarmingly frank manner.

The first thing she tells me is that the nun who normally runs
the abbey is on sick leave with chronic fatigue syndrome. This
strikes me as a strange affliction for a Buddhist spiritual leader; only
good breeding prevents me from bringing it up. She writes her
name for me: Alika Pietrzy Kokski. She is Polish, a clinical psychol-
ogist from Warsaw who arrived in Canada in 1967 when her ex-
husband landed a teaching post at the University of Waterloo in
Ontario.

"We had lived all over the world, in Brazil, Africa and Edinburgh,"
she says. "I had everything most people would want—a Mercedes,
a swimming pool, clothes from Paris—and I was very unhappy. I
did not know then that happiness is a state of mind. I just felt there
was something more. I began training with the Gestalt Institute in
Toronto. I trained with native Americans. Then I trained on an

eight-week program in Buddhism in 1975. I had no doubt that this was the path for me. Then I met Trungpa Rinpoche in Vermont. That's how it all started." She was ordained in 1982 and has been a nun for thirteen years. The path, as the Buddhists like to say, is not an easy one. Just temporarily taking the robes of a monk or nun means living in Gampo Abbey for at least six months. Another eighteen months of work and study and you can take a novice's vows. A year later and you are allowed the full vows of a monk.

For a second I am worried that just showing up here for a visit means that I've inadvertently committed myself to three months in the lotus position. For time did sound like it passed slowly at Gampo Abbey. Today is Sunday, for example. That means up at 6, meditation from 6:30 till 7:30, breakfast, free time, more meditation from 8:30 to 11, then complete silence until noon. After a vegetarian lunch the afternoon is spent working in the gardens or around the site. Another meditation session from 5 till 6, a vegetarian dinner, then more meditation from 7 until 8. Everyone is in bed and prohibited from saying a word from 10 on. "Everyone follows the given Buddhist precepts—refrain from killing, lying, stealing, sexual activity and taking intoxicants or drugs," Palmo says, adding, with a faint smile, "The local people think we are strange but harmless."

No kidding. As we walk through the hall she introduces me to a huge, bald, menacing-looking man in robes, the abbey's financial officer. I can just imagine him pulling into the service station at nearby Pleasant Bay, rolling down the window and saying "Please fill it up" to some high-school altar boy who thinks Protestants are exotic. Today the only noise in the abbey is the wind, which roars off the Gulf of St. Lawrence, bending the trees sideways. T. Palmo, who suffers from emphysema and moves with difficulty, shows me the spacious kitchen, the well-stocked library, the simple, pleasant rooms where the nuns and monks live.

I am asked to remove my shoes before entering the shrine room. Inside are the sacred texts, bowls of offering water, the Tibetan gongs and cymbals. From there I can look outside and I see a woman meditating on a bench overlooking the curving bay and the ocean. I ask Palmo if she's found what she was looking for here. "It is very personal," she says with a shrug. "I am happy. All of life is preparation for death anyway."

I look back out the window; the bench is empty. All I can see is, well, everything. To some the view may be a blank space. To the Buddhists, and the other seekers who end up here, the air vibrates with possibility. It shows where they've been and also where they are going.

Eleven

Home for Sale

—

LET ME BE CLEAR ON THIS: I HAD TO LIE. THERE WAS NO WAY AROUND IT. Otherwise I would have been ripping down the highway heading southwest from Halifax with no place to start. And even for this whole deluded enterprise that would have been unthinkable.

"So, Demo, you have done some sailing, right?"

"Absolutely, Leroy," I responded before launching into this long line about how I crewed with the Murphy brothers back in the early 1980s, and how we came second in the Maritimes in some obscure regatta series. Which was true. There was, as I saw it, no reason to tell the skipper of *Third Wave* that I had been mere ballast—170 pounds of flesh and bone to keep the boat from capsizing. That if, under the rules, they could have used a tackling dummy or maybe a boulder instead of bringing me along they would have.

"You know your way around a boat, then?"

"Oh, yeah, of course. And at the very least I can follow orders." I tried to inject what I imagined was a devil-may-care quality into my voice. "Shit, you don't have to worry. I won't get in anyone's way."

So now I was a yachtsman, competing in a series of races held in the pretty little village of Chester. I like the sound of being a *yachtsman*. It calls up visions of bow to bow on the high seas, popping spinnakers in gale-force winds, coming about as million-dollar sailboats speed alongside, then back to the harbour at dusk for a tray of rum-and-Cokes, tall, family-sized drinks reclining on some rich guy's deck, while supermodels in Thurston Howell III hats giggle as they play croquet on the lawn below. So what if Leroy let me come aboard only for one day? I am still a yachtsman; that is my story and I am sticking to it. Because I seriously doubt that a person can spend a day in a better way than on a Philadelphia stockbroker's boat zipping along at foolish speeds through gorgeous Mahone Bay. But also because I am on a subversive mission—to see if it is really possible to buy home.

It would be easy if that were the case. Just find a place that suits your desires and then, if you have enough money, open up the chequebook. An interesting question to consider in Nova Scotia where it takes, let's see, three or four generations living here before your family are not considered newcomers and where all manner of rich Germans, well-heeled Americans, Ontarians with too much disposable income have recently arrived on their individual quests. At some point the newcomers may run the risk of spoiling the very nature of the place they came in search of. But Nova Scotia is probably just too far from the rest of the world to make that a worry. Right now the issue is more immediate and fundamental: the nature of connecting with a place and its people. In other words, finding home, then holding on to it.

Chester is the kind of spot where you need a cover story.

Otherwise, try sidling up to some zinc-nosed member of the idle rich at the bar at the Chester Yacht Club and babbling about your thrilling job behind the cheese counter at Sobey's and see how far that gets you. Me, on the other hand, I am a yachtsman. Which means something else altogether. The peculiar thing is that Chester, for all its antique social system of caste and privilege, looks like a bit of a backwater on the way in. Two-lane blacktop shaded by trees, a few signs advertising motels and gift shops with the usual bogus nautical names. The voice on the car radio promises "highs in the mid-twenties, with moderate seas and a light chop on coastal waters." Is that good or bad for sailing? I drive along a narrow road, over a twisting hill and—Wow, it's like I've suddenly descended into this cool, shaded garden. I slow down. Wind jostles the branches overhead, letting fingers of sunlight filter through. Manicured hedges line the narrow, quiet streets. Behind all the foliage I glimpse grand homes with signs and brass plates bearing elevated names like Morning Tide, Pinecroft, Westerleigh, Sand Castle, Over the Way. I pass a rambling white three-storey bar-restaurant, the Captain's House, which I read somewhere is all that's left of the grand hotels from the old days.

Nearby I park my rust-encrusted 1988 Toyota next to a lot full of Bimmers, Saabs and Land Rovers. I love my car for the simple reason that it looks like it has nothing to lose. If the owner of a Jaguar, say, arrives at one of those traffic circles where everyone is supposed to alternate turns and sees my thing coming across, well you just know who's going to be slamming on the brakes. So I'm fully prepared for somebody's butler to come out and put the run on me. Nothing happens, though. Which I take as a fine omen. I walk past a plaque from Norwegian seamen who convalesced there during the war years and step up into the stand where the Chester Brass Band performs. From here I can see the artless old yacht club, the tufted Ice Age islands that dot the bay, and the narrow neck of the Peninsula, an exclusive little lick of land that separates Front Harbour from Back Harbour.

Exactly a year earlier I stood here taking in the same view. Then I took a little walk over to where Charles Ritchie lived. Now there was a man: a suave, witty diplomat who walked in the world's highest circles as the ambassador to the United Nations and London during the golden years of the Canadian foreign service. I knew him more for his Governor General's Award–winning diaries, within which I seem to remember him writing the sentence "In the afternoon I dined on capon and read a pornographic book in the library." At eighty-seven he was bald and so cadaverously thin that I could see his ribs through his white dress shirt. Yet sitting there amongst his books, bony knees crossed, mind dancing like wind chimes, he was exactly what I expected. "There's a timeless quality to this place, a most agreeable rhythm of parties, entertaining and informal visits which you find yourself falling into," he told me. Most of all I remembered how he hated the way old age was cutting into his partygoing. When I left he was arguing good-naturedly with his housekeeper about the time. "No, my dear, your watch is fifteen minutes slow," I heard him say as I let myself out. "It is twelve o'clock. Which means it *is* time for my glass of wine."

But he died a week ago; mortality even in this timeless place. It is only a short walk along the water to a comfortable wooden house called the Quarterdeck. Desmond Piers leads me inside. Everyone I asked said I should visit him because he is the man to see about Chester's social history. The perfect omniscient narrator, I was told, charming, wise, the ancient keeper of all its secrets. Piers has summered here every year since 1916, except during World War Two, when as a rear admiral he commanded destroyers and won the Distinguished Service Cross during the Battle of the Atlantic. He had an even better life afterwards: chairman of the Canadian Joint Staff in Washington, Canada's military representative to NATO and the principal military adviser to the Canadian ambassador in Washington. Piers, I learn, is eighty-two. He wears his wavy hair combed back and has the tan and smile of an old-time Hollywood leading man. Today, he sports a yellow short-sleeved shirt and green pants and looks like he just shot a quick eighteen at the Chester Golf Club.

Actually, he's going once I stop bothering him. First, though, I need to know something about Chester in the old days. It's like throwing on a switch. "Oh, it was a well-founded place with a vibrant, vital local population when the summer people came," he gushes. "The well-to-do Americans who discovered Chester wanted somewhere beautiful where they could escape the heat of the big cities. The trout and salmon fishing was wonderful. They came and built houses with shady verandahs. Nearly every family had a yacht to race and a tennis court. They hired unemployed Chester boys to look after their properties. But there was no ostentation. They were quiet and discreet."

He knows everything. How a boatload of New Englanders arrived in the mid-1700s to settle a tongue of land sheltered in Mahone Bay. How a century later John Wister, a wealthy stove manufacturer from Philadelphia, arrived on a summer vacation and bought a property he made into a summer home christened Wisteria. How other wealthy Americans followed: the Starrs and the Pews (heirs to the Sun Oil fortune) from Philadelphia; the Trimbles, the Carrolls, the Finneys, from Baltimore; the Groves of St. Louis; Gen. Rutherford Bingham, a veteran of the Spanish-American War and the former police commissioner of New York City, the presidents of Princeton and Rutgers, the U.S. ambassador to Russia.

He tells me about the golf club, built by a Scottish lumber merchant just for the rich summer people. And how Colonel Something-or-other buried his wife and son along the third hole. He tells me about the war years and how the mix started to change here as more Upper Canadians and well-off Haligonians began to summer in Chester. He tells me how magazine writers are always coming around to do stories about the animosity between the summer folk and the year-rounders—and how they always leave empty-handed. "Oh, everyone gets along here quite nicely," he says with a smile, his fingers laced contentedly behind his head. "It is really extraordinary."

Does he somehow know that when I leave here I'm heading

back along the harbour and up the winding climb past the high hedges, the impenetrable gates and No Trespassing signs to the very end of the Peninsula? As I manoeuvre up the hill I can almost hear them behind the gates, harrumphing about liberals, capital gains taxes and how Helms-Burton has thrown the market for Cubanos out of whack. The gals, I imagine, with Kate Hepburn tough-girl nicknames like Babs and Slim, with Jackie O. hairstyles and memories of dancing with some long-ago beau to "String of Pearls" before he went off and bought it on the beaches of Normandy. The menfolk slumming it in their ascots and blazers, clutching a tall gin-and-tonic as they reminisce about how they could have bought IBM at three bucks a share.

All of which gives a refreshingly arriviste quality to the man who greets me at the top. Tim Moore wears a T-shirt, khakis, topsiders and Lillehammer '94 ball cap, the midmorning sun glinting off the gold in his watch, chunky wrist bracelet and thin neck chain. "There was a lot of talk in town, perhaps because of the size of the house," he explains when we sit down. "Crazy talk about me being part of the Mafia, stuff like that. Then *Venture* did a piece. I was on Gzowski. *Frank* started writing about us. It got to the point where I didn't know anyone but everyone knew me and what I did."

Moore is in the moving business; his company, A.M.J. Campbell Van Lines, does $65 million a year in sales; it is based in Toronto, but he keeps a fax, phone and computer humming on the third floor of his Chester home and once a week drives into Halifax and flies to head office. I've heard and read his name lots since moving back. The house was the main reason. More for what it symbolized to a certain slice of Chester gentry than anything else: the new, the slightly showy, the lack of respect for tradition. Sure, Moore had money, *but what kind?* When the Peninsula crowd think of *real* Chester wealth they think of old money, passed down like the fine houses themselves, from generation to generation. The remnants of the longest-established aristocratic summer families may be losing interest in making the long drive from Philadelphia or Baltimore. They may, in fact, start cranking martinis as soon as it gets dark under the front porch. But Moore—he is a *trucker,* for God's sake!

"Life in Toronto used to be full of stresses," he reflects when I ask what brought him here. "When I wasn't in the office or on the 401 I was on an airplane. That is the danger in being financially successful: once you achieve a certain level of net worth you feel you have to go out and get more and more and more." But his wife is a Maritimer; they honeymooned in Chester eighteen years ago. So when it came time to try to shift lifestyle gears, a real estate agent told them about this property. Moore laid down half a mil, subdivided the land, kept the best chunk for himself and recouped the costs by selling the rest. The people on the Peninsula, he says, were a collective pain in the ass, particularly the group from Halifax: they wouldn't let him subdivide; they complained about the trucks going up and down the road; because of them he had to pay an extra $40,000 to hook up the power.

Now we're sitting in the backyard of his eight-year-old home on his five-and-one-half-acre property. It is a mansion, really, with fifteen-foot ceilings, gold-glinting bathroom fixtures and an aqua swimming pool shimmering in the trees and groomed gardens. The view, much as I try, is what I cannot take my eyes off: 270 degrees of blue, sun-burst water; a handful of candy-spinnakered sailboats; a Cape Islander steaming out to the open ocean—like stepping into a Leroy Neiman. Dead ahead, the bulk of Quaker Island. Swivel your head to the right and sprawling Cape Cods, pillared Georgian mansions shaded by the pines and birches, their lawns unrolling like carpets to the ocean. To the left, the bay, leading to the emerald golf course, where a wicked slice could take out a German orthodontist in a powerboat.

Everybody said the view from Moore's back lawn is the best anywhere on the basin, better than financier, author and adventurer Chris Ondaatje's or that of Mariellen Black, Monty's ex-wife, or former federal Tory finance minister Barbara McDougall's, or Don Johnston's (the head of the OECD, not the ageing hunk-boy actor) or even from the huge property Brandon Stoddard, the Hollywood producer, is building on Rafuse Island. No one knew for certain if Moore's house is at the moment the biggest or the most grandly furnished in house-proud Chester. It's certainly the most talked about.

It is curious to hear what else people are talking about in this incestuous, snobbish, gossipy little spot. I drive down to the yacht club, chat up a woman working the bar and pry a few words out of a reticent sort on the race committee. Ritchie's death comes up. So does the romance between an ageing village matron and a young jazz musician, the battle over whether to change the name of Pig Loop Rd., the $4-million, 30,000-square-foot house lobster baron John Risley was building near the golf course and the usual rumours about mysterious Germans and Hollywood moguls buying islands in Mahone Bay.

It is noon now and the yacht club crowd is already getting it on. Over at the bar some big guys with ruddy complexions are guzzling Coke with guvy—that's Governor General's rum for the uninitiated—with two hands. People who look like they have been ripped right from the pages of a J. Crew catalogue—khaki shorts, cableknit sweaters, yellow rubber boots—hug each other and shake hands with big grins and a whoop here and there. "By God, you old bastard! Good to see you. *Damn good,* and I *mean* it." Young peacocks, sunglasses hanging from around their necks on little black strings, strut around sizing up the competition. Some good-looking women: groupies? local society belles? There are even serious sailors, eyeing the computer printouts on the wall that carry the day's draw. Jimmy Buffett, the patron saint of all seagoing types, wafts from the sound system. Out back, the Johnny-on-the-Spots stand in a green, glistening row, a few yards from the big, inflatable beer dirigibles.

Walking by a window, I check my disguise: I am wearing a blue-and-white-striped sweatshirt, which has a faintly nautical air. I have on bone-white mail-order shorts and Rockport deck shoes with no socks. A baseball hat sits atop my head. About then I notice my skipper heading down the wharf carrying a bunch of gear. "Deemoooo," Leroy, whose real name is John Roy, chants when he sees me. As well as making a good living peddling yachts to rich guys, he is one of the best racing captains around. So I'm trying not to think about how he'll react once he realizes I can't sail even a bit.

The rest of the crew is already here: an engineer, a mutual fund salesman, the manager of a sail outfitter, a phone company lineman and an insurance dealer. They bullshit back and forth, cracking tasteless O.J. jokes, razzing each other about wives and girlfriends, recounting tired stories of long-ago drinking bouts that always end with somebody puking on a cop's shoes. They enjoy the easy familiarity of having worked in close quarters hundreds of times, and raced Chester together probably every year since their voices broke. A motor launch putt-putt-putts alongside and the yacht owner, Clarence "Binky" Wurts, and his son, Charlie, climb aboard. Everyone is pulling on ropes, hauling sails and speaking in racing-boat code. "Whoa," somebody yells in warning as the boom swings for my head. I turn around and see a couple of crewmen eyeing me suspiciously. The owner of a yacht supply store in Halifax sidles up beside me.

"How much racing have you done, John?" he asks. I launch into my story. He listens as he coils rope, then places it neatly by a rail.

"The boat has three sections," he says matter-of-factly. "Frontier land, adventure land and fantasy land." Adventure land—sort of this middle ground between the cockpit and the bow where, I assumed, it was felt I would be less of a headache—had become my domain.

■ ■ ■

Regattas, according to the official race program, have been held in Chester since 1856, when thousands of people raced in everything from canoes to sailboats and the prizes were "flour, sugar, hats or money." Now the winners of the Chester Race Week regatta get silver cups. But the whole thing still has an air of shabby gentility about it, from the ninety-five-year-old yacht club, once somebody's boathouse, to the heavy brass cannon, which eighty-eight-year-old Ben Heisler is struggling to ignite aboard the race boat to begin the day's racing. I've eyeballed Heisler, the legendary boat builder, close up. He looks like one of those apple dolls, all wrinkles and weathered skin. I also know that after thirty years of performing this task he has gone stone deaf and gets through the ritual only with hefty rations of rum and Coke. All of which makes me wonder, as *Third Wave* circles the race committee boat and I watch him struggle with the cannon: is this man actually being allowed to handle a loaded firearm?

But he pulls it off without incident, God bless him. A crisp, northerly breeze as *Third Wave,* a C&C 37, shoots past the starting line a half-mile off the Chester waterfront. We tack a couple of times and I manage to do a few menial tasks without incident. Next thing, we're bearing down on this narrow island.

"It's a crapshoot," complains Leroy.

He bets the best air lies to the right. Soon as we come around it our sails sag impotently as we watch the boats who tacked left spread the gap. An uncomfortable silence settles over the boat.

Leroy glowers from beneath the *Third Wave* hat pulled low on his forehead. Binky, who owns a Philadelphia stock brokerage, just sits at the stern, his thin lips pinched together. His son, Charlie, a Wall Street stockbroker, pulls on ropes and mutters under his breath. The rest of the crew sit, crouch and lay at their stations. Just a boat full of dead eyes searching for a breath of wind. The mood is ugly; mutiny hovers in the air as we marvel at how the lead boat in our class has managed to get so far out ahead in such a short time. Then everybody kind of says what the hell and surrenders to the weather and the day's high spirits. They try some fancy spinnaker work, coming around the last mark. Then amuse themselves on the run in by popping beers, dangling their legs over the side, and passing around the binoculars to ogle an all-women's boat.

Somebody decreed that no negative words could pass anyone's lips for the rest of the race. The only real test came when I am ordered below to pull in sail as it is dropped. I haul like all get-out. But it just keeps coming and coming. It seems to be filling the cabin and I can't keep up with it. Then I'm ensnared. I try to claw myself free, jabbering a great string of obscenities, stumble sideways and land on the floor in this writhing, sweaty mass. I'm gulping for air when my head finally emerges from the white shroud. In the hatch directly overhead I see a face—I don't know whose—and hear the words: "Good sail work."

We finish eleventh out of fourteen boats in our class. But it's just Monday and everything is full of promise as we tie up next to the yacht club wharf. An aria from *Madame Butterfly* floats from the cabin of another straggler motoring in. Binky Wurts, the seventh generation of his family to summer in Chester, cracks a can of Keith's and sits down in the cockpit. He's fifty-four, tanned, thin, athletic looking, with what can only be described as a country-club face—straight nose, aristocratically tiny ears that hug the head. "Do you know Danny Blaine?" he asks me. "Well, his grandfather, my grandfather and another were the first Wisters who came here. I came here for the first time as a child in 1947. We'd stay at the old Lovett House hotel. My grandmother ended up owning it during the recession. We've bought and sold various houses over the years. Now we're in Chandler's Cove, off the golf course. Charlie was five years old when he first came. He grew up here. I don't think there is a prettier bay anywhere in the world. Every inlet or island has a sandy beach. The temperature is perfect. Coming back here is like being on a honeymoon: all our friends come down, we open our houses up, we go fishing, we play golf and tennis, we watch the sunset."

By the clubhouse a pleasant post-coital mood has settled over the sailors and hangers-on sipping beer in plastic cups as they relive the race. "You bastard, we had ya. Lord Christ, we did. Helluvaday, though, *helluvaday!* Here, what're ya having, beer? Chrissakes, let me get you a real drink." From the sound system Peter Tosh exhorts the world to lively up yourself. I get a drink and wander out on the deck. My face feels sunburned and I've got that little weave going that always afflicts landlubbers who've just spent an unaccustomed amount of time aboard a boat. Leroy, who is talking to some people on the grass, raises his glass at me in some sort of salute. Meaning unknown.

I spend a few minutes hovering around. Finally I see someone I've met before, an American who once told me he "did well during the Reagan years." He winters in Florida and spends summers in Chester in a home that has been in the family for more than a century. His face wears that ruddy flushed look you so often see in photos on the walls of golf and yacht clubs. I blather on for a bit about the day's conditions, and other subjects that seem to interest sailors. He skitters away, leaving me with the owner of a local marina. A nice guy. He stands there in the sun, this thick globe of zinc oxide on his nose, and informs me that every boat in the Chester fleet has a nickname and then runs through them. To my mind, the best one is *Turd Wave,* but I could be biased.

My bed-and-breakfast is a pleasant walk away. I change my clothes, then stroll back to the water and follow the harbour to a bar and restaurant called the Rope Loft. Rope stanchions, cork buoys, pocked driftwood, other nautica. I make for the deck and a table all to myself, then watch a boatful of latecomers stumble down the gangplank. By the looks of it they've had a day. Takes them a good thirty seconds to stagger the few yards from the gangplank. A man and a woman cling to each other to avoid falling down—bank execs, no doubt, here at the invitation of their regional manager, who follows with a flat frozen grin as he watches an elaborate attempt to suck up to superiors disappear amidst the hangovers and recriminations to come.

Almost eight when I pay the cheque. Up the hill to the Fo'c'sle Tavern, which is the real thing, not some nautical theme bar. The first time I was here a husky little trawlerman clutching handfuls of money growled at me like a wolverine. Tonight the big amiable bouncer says I'm early for the real excitement. So I wander back to the yacht club just as the day's racing prizes are being handed out. Lots of warm, good-spirited laughter. Two of the recipients have to be pushed up to receive their hardware. One is so blasted he can't even string a sentence together and just waves his little trophy over his head.

A four-piece cover band sets up at the back of the clubhouse. Then starts banging out tunes by Janis Joplin, the Beatles and the other icons of sixties rock and roll. The room fills up. A woman, mistaking me for my doctor cousin, grabs me by the arm. I try to make chitchat with a wealthy heiress, who spends the whole time searching for eye contact over my shoulder with a Johnny Depp lookalike half her age.

By now the social strata has settled. Most of the real money is at home, inside the elegant old homes I pass walking back up the hill. Inside the Fo'c'sle the stockbrokers, management consultants, lawyers, doctors and trust fund babies swarm the bar, pounding back endless glasses of draught and guvy-and-Coke. They strike me as a smug, almost boring lot. But I'm an outsider looking in. I get the impression this is their sacred place: that when they come here to crank a few during Race Week it is always when things were good, when anything seemed possible. Before divorce, corporate downsizings, male pattern baldness, twelve-step programs and easy-fit jeans. Before the wife's high-school sweetheart started getting mentioned in the *RoB* and Gretzky headed stateside. Before light beer, Robert Bly and nice, sensible mini-vans.

So Chester is one thing to them and another to the townies in the corner, sticking to themselves, a bit overwhelmed, maybe a touch resentful of the invading preppy hordes with their designer labels and this band they've never seen before, in their bar, playing a tune by someone called Hootie and the Blowfish. I lurch in their direction to hear what they think. And it is precisely then that I meet the two biggest bores in all of the South Shore of Nova Scotia.

"You want to know about Chester Race Week, this here's your man," says the blonde woman, whom I would put at about university age, clinging fiercely to the arm of the older guy. His face has a funny saggy quality, which could be from age, booze or indifference. Listening to this pair go on about his skill behind the tiller was just too much. I lie about having to get a refill, do a little broken-field running through the crowd of strutting drunks, and slip out the exit.

It's around twelve-thirty when I make one last visit to the yacht club on the way home. Inside, a lanky blond-haired sailor, no doubt half-crazed from too much sun and rum, steps up to the drum set and begins banging along with the band to something by Creedence Clearwater Revival. Finding his rhythm, he gets this goofy little smile as his friends cheer him on and I watch through the smoke. It is, even by the standards of the day, a nice moment.

Turning a corner outside, I run into Ben Heisler, walking on stiff legs but still going strong, off to God knows where. A white MG convertible drives by like a ghost. In the dark, waves lap the shore and the inky water planes to Europe. Somewhere in the distance there is laughter.

A couple of days later I'm back in Chester, this time with a friend. Once a left-winger for the Edmonton Oilers, Brian McKenzie now sells real estate. He used to keep his powerboat anchored in a near-by cove until the recession caught up to him. So he knows exactly what to do when we wheel up to the wharf in Chester and see a hundred or so people waiting to make the 45-minute one-dollar ferry ride to Big Tancook Island. When we pull into the Oak Island marina a few minutes later a shirtless, tanned guy with a truly mon-umental gut waves a greeting. Before a half-hour is passed we're aboard a fully loaded powerboat cutting into the bay.

Our captain looks mangled and bent; horrible, horrible. He must have groaned in agony when he rolled over in his bunk this morn-ing, searched vainly for a drop of moisture in what was once his mouth and felt the mule kick the inside of his cranium. It was still, no doubt, a little blurry. Barry—which is what we'll call him for now—would have been suffering through the please-God-I'll-never-do-it-again part of his hangover when he remembered that the pre-vious night ended a couple of wharfs away with a woman throwing a drink in his face and him weaving back to his own boat for a screaming match with the wife who, by now, was back home in

Halifax. Still, it is noon and with each passing minute the night mercifully fades further into history. Helps that he is steaming away from
the marina under a sunny sky at a nice fifteen-knot clip, dressed in
cutoffs and a tank top, a family-sized rum-and-Coke in hand, Alan
Jackson's nasal twang blaring from the loudspeaker. He even manages a weak smile when he turns to peer red-eyed from behind his
sunglasses at us, the intruders in his bout of self-flagellation.

I have never been on Big Tancook, but retain a vivid image of it
anyway, pieced together from stories I'd heard. They make sauerkraut and build wonderful schooners, the fame of both having
spread far beyond the area. They forge a hard but good living as
farmers and fishermen. They are known to be an insular bunch,
speaking a dialogue that is indecipherable, even by South Shore
standards. After my day aboard *Third Wave* I became obsessed with
the idea of the island out there a few miles from all this wealth. By
the time we drop anchor the ferry has just docked and the main
road, which arcs along the island's main anchorage and continues
up a hill, swarms with people. We step into the slipstream and follow the crowd past the small wharfs and launchways, the remnants
of the old fish houses, the ruins of the underground cabbage cellars,
the tables on the front lawns piled with the quilts and baked goods.

Chester Race Week may be one thing, Tancook's annual Herring
Chokers Picnic, the highlight of *their* summer, most definitely
another. The old-time country band is just finishing a set of hurting
music at the recreation centre at the top of the hill. I recognize the
leader—Sherman "Little Buddy" Hirtle, short, round and sixtyish,

resplendent in his red shirt, string tie and white cowboy hat. As we approach he lays down his guitar and ambles towards the white hall, where awaits heaping bowls of fish chowder, biscuits, kraut, plates of herring and potatoes, tables full of homemade pies, cakes, squares and cookies and pots of tea and coffee. The crowd outside sits on benches, lawnchairs and the grass. My eyes are drawn to the cars parked near the hall, held together with string, duct tape and chicken wire, missing doors, with rusted-out skeletons for frames. I half-expect some leather-encased Mad Max reject to climb from the rubble and fire up his chainsaw. Most lack licence plates, which is no surprise, since you don't need insurance or even mainland registration to drive on Tancook. One plate dates back to 1976 and comes from Newfoundland.

I have been on Tancook for only forty minutes but already I recognize the genre: an outlying island of unfashionable and out-of-step people, best appreciated for their dramatic art of self-preservation. I jot down a few notes. Brian appears with a woman in tow who asks if I want to meet one of the last sauerkraut makers on the island. A few minutes later I'm sandwiched between Percy and Evelyn in their half-ton. Already, I'm confused.

"Before you start I said last year I was never going to have any more interviews any more in my life," says the husband in a slightly accusatory tone. "What happened there was a fellow I talked to him and he published something I never said, some hurtful things. He said that I was supposed to say that all of the other factories, their kraut tasted like straw. I wouldn't say anything like that about anybody. So I said I'm finished with interviews."

"I felt really upset about it, you know what I mean," says Evelyn. "We're just little. We just do this as a hobby. We're not that big, you know."

Hoping to cool the old guy down, I ask Percy who showed him how to make sauerkraut.

"Who? From the time I could walk and talk, my father and grandfather. My father and grandfather planted cabbage through the years and it just felt natural to grow it. This was the way people made a living. It was part of their lives and their livelihood. When I grew up it was fishing and farming. I fished entirely for a living from the time I was fourteen until I was forty-nine, then I went to work on that ferry. I'm seventy-seven now. I worked there until I was sixty-five. These last twelve years we plant cabbage and make sauerkraut."

His weather-ravaged face relaxes a bit as he tells me the old way of making kraut. How they sow the cabbage seeds, then transplant, fertilize and spray them until they grow to fifteen to twenty-five pounds. How they ferment them for twelve days in salt water. And how they finally pack them in open pails—ten, twenty and thirty gallons large—before sale. "It's something special, like the Lunenburg sausage, passed down from generation to generation," he explains. "But now only Arthur Stevens and myself do it. We're the last of the Tancook kraut makers."

As I thank them and take my leave, the music is starting up again. From halfway up the hill I turn back for a last look at what they see: the hang-dog cars, the once-thriving farmland overgrown with briers, the population of a thousand now shrunk to a few hundred, the working-aged men who'd be on welfare if not for UI. Onshore, if you've got the name and the money, maybe you can buy home. Here maybe even that is not enough. Evelyn's words echo: "This is a little island and a way of life. This is where I was born. It is home; we think it is special."

Being over-dressed happens rarely to someone who wears what I do—someone who, if the occasion really demands, will upgrade from casual to dress jeans. But here I am, luminous in my chinos and linen jacket in the midst of this sea of topsiders, golf shirts and Bermuda shorts. There are many social gaucheries, of course. But short of admitting to membership in the United Aryan Brotherhood, over-dressing is up there. Truth is, wear a Grateful Dead T-shirt or one of those Rasta tea-cosy hats to a Chester cocktail party and people will probably think you're somebody's software genius son, or a movie producer scouting for a spot to stand in for Martha's Vineyard in their new Hollywood romantic comedy. Wear a sportscoat to Tim Moore's open house on the last day of Chester Race Week, on the other hand ...

"Lose the jacket and you'll be fine," whispers a sympathetic woman I know slightly, today sporting jeans and a faded denim shirt instead of the power suit and pumps she wears back in Halifax. We're nursing beers on Moore's huge back lawn, standing as far as possible from the huge fat-spitting barbecue. Her boyfriend, a yacht outfitter who crewed on *Third Wave,* tells me how their bad luck ended when I stepped off the boat; overall, they're second on the week, and they had a great crew party at Binky's house, which culminated at midnight with the bunch of them driving golf balls from his lawn onto the fairways of the Chester course next door.

Moore's party really marks the end of Race Week and, in a way, the end of summer in the village. Soon the beautiful people will be gone and Chester will return to its normal, everyday self. Right now, though, cars clog the lane leading to the house; a gaggle of kids frolic in the pool; most of the adults stand out back drinking wine and beer, trying to fit their mouths around monster hamburgers while they ooh and aah at the thirty or forty boats tacking out of the bay, directly in front of them. It all seems so perfect, the sharply coloured sails billowing in the wind, the sun, the ocean, the healthy-looking, happy people taking their leisure. I sink down in a chair on the sweeping verandah, next to a balding guy with a grey beard, sunglasses and a blinding shirt hanging over his shorts. Jose Valverde Alcalde moved from his native Spain to Canada in 1964 to teach art at the University of Calgary. Now he lives half the year near Barcelona and the rest of the time in Chester, where he fuses hot Spanish colours with images of the South Shore in his brilliantly coloured paintings. We chat for a minute. Then he excuses himself. "I have to take some pictures of the boats," he explains. I watch him walk away, his shirt floating like a spinnaker in the breeze.

"Who's that?" a former Mulroney cabinet minister who's been summering in Chester since he was a child asks no one in particular.

"A painter," a white-haired swell standing nearby replies. "Jose Alcado."

"Alcado. Alcado. What kind of a name is that?"

"Spanish, I think."

"Sounds like Dildo to me," spits the ex-politician, now back to practising law, before bursting into loud, humourless laughter.

I get back into my beater and make my way down the hill away from the Peninsula.

PART FOUR

Being There

A few homesick men, walking an alien street;

A few women remembering misty stars

And the long grumbling sigh of the bay at night.

Charles Bruce

———

Twelve

In Blood Is Meaning

———

HIGHWAY 4 BETWEEN SYDNEY AND GLACE BAY IS WHERE I HAVE MY VISION. It hits quick and hard—an image in my mind's eye of a cloudless day, a serene green cemetery and a four-year-old watching his father wiping away a single rivulet of tear. It has enough power to make me pull a sudden U-turn and head back, the car rumbling and groaning as the speedometer crosses 120 km/h. The woman minding the office at Forest Haven Memorial Gardens takes a few minutes to search the files, then hands me a map of the cemetery. I take my time walking across the well-tended grass so closely cut that it resembles a golf green. I pick my way through the rows of gravestones until I reach lot number 108 B. The markers are identical— polished bronze, each with a carving of an open Bible near the top. Only enough room to say that Clarence Demont (he never capitalized the *m*) died on September 14, 1959, at age sixty-six and Mabel, his wife, was seventy-eight when she died on September 6, 1975.

I already knew that. What is noteworthy is that I had been here just once before, thirty-six years ago. Furthermore, I never knew the name of the place where my grandparents lay buried. All I had was a nagging, vague memory, which hadn't flashed through my mind in years until a few minutes ago. A true Daphne du Maurier moment. I feel a grand gesture of some kind is in order, but I cannot, for the life of me, think of the right one. All I can say is it feels wholly natural to stand staring at the ground, hands sunk deep in my pockets, nostrils twitching from summer pollen, my feet rooted to the soil and the vanished generations.

I don't normally let this sort of thing preoccupy me. Like everyone in the late twentieth century, I know that self-determination is the Zeitgeist of the moment. We all make our story up as we go along. We all live on our wits, not our past. But you can't escape it either, no matter how hard you try. It is what bolts you to the earth. Particularly if you are suspicious of the Christian belief in heaven and hell and have no confidence whatsoever that a saviour was ever in sight. In blood can be found meaning—like all Nova Scotians, I firmly believe that. When you come from here, where roots run so deeply, it is easy to take that for granted. Then something will drive it home—that you are still just a small root from a great tree descending deep into the black, coal-laden soil.

It happened to me at a funeral for an ancient great-aunt, Eva Mount, a smart, lively woman I remembered for her Sunday dinners and organ playing as much as for her spirit and sharpness of mind. There I sat thinking how much the scene resembled some forty-year-old film footage I've seen, in which many of the same people sat in a church in Sydney Mines watching the nervous overheated couple who became my parents take their wedding vows.

Clarence Demont, my grandfather, was a newspaper printer and church hall janitor in his working days. He was a fidgety man, with a bald head, long, downward-sloping nose and gentle eyes. But his double-breasted suit hid the remnants of a body that could once out-sprint racehorses, pin barn-storming wrestling champions and run down any flyball in the outfield. He could have gone to the Olympics, been the Donovan Bailey of his day. But, family legend has it, his boss in the composing room at the Glace Bay *Gazette* couldn't promise him his job when he returned. And since a job was nothing to sneeze at in Depression-era Cape Breton he stayed in Glace Bay. No one found him a resentful man: shy in public, Clarie "Flash" Demont was a live wire in private, a Baptist with a high-pitched laugh who danced with a loosey-goosey up-and-down movement of the arms as he expelled air through pursed lips to some far-away rhythm only he heard.

I was just a toddler when he died so I have not a single actual memory of him—just stories from my father. And a few mementoes: an aged, leather-bound copy of *Wild Wales: The People's Language & Scenery* by George Borrow, on the title page of which is written:"1st place 100 yards dash won by Clarence Demont, July 31/19 Knox Church Sunday School Picnic." I also have a black-and-white photo of when he was in his prime, wearing shorts, an athletic top and sprinter's spikes, legs and arms flexed ready to propel him forward to some unseen finish line.

Across the aisle in 1955 my mother's father sat, straight-backed, sober looking, smelling of pipe tobacco and English tweed. John Briers was a kid when his father left the coal fields of Yorkshire and crossed the Atlantic to work the collieries of Cape Breton. Like all good sons he followed his father underground, working a coal face that ran miles out under the water. When war broke out he enlisted in Montreal and saw action at Vimy Ridge. British to the core, he was not one to dwell on the horrors he experienced overseas. When World War Two began he enlisted again. Back in Cape Breton, he spent his days in the darkness of the mines, eventually rising to the level of inspector. But after a day on the job, a big English-style dinner and a nap, he headed for the parlour, where he rosined up the bow for his violin or played the piano, saxophone or clarinet into the night. Long decades later old women still shivered with pleasure at the memory of his alto sax floating across the water at dances at the Sydney Mines Yacht Club.

I own his saxophone now, or at least a refurbished version, which Lisa presented me on my thirtieth birthday. It is a made by the legendary C.G. Conn Ltd. of Elkhart, Ind. One of my sax teachers told me he thought it was a Chu Berry model (named after the American saxophone player Leon "Chu" Berry), which meant it was probably made in the late 1920s. I have been playing it, on and off and poorly, for at least a decade now. I am acutely aware that the inlay in the keys—where I fumble to place my fingers—has been worn down over time by my grandfather's hands. Few days go by during which I do not think about how I now struggle to force lungfuls of air down the same valves he breathed into for so long. The instrument sits in my office in a battered black case a few feet away from a photocopy of a brief notice in the Toronto *Star*. It says:

"Clarie Demont, 66, once the fastest Canadian to run 100 yards, died in Glace Bay, N.S., yesterday. His mark of 9.6 seconds in the 100-yard was set in 1913."

And thus am I reminded every day of my closeness to the past and the vast gulf separating me from my predecessors. I spend most of my day talking to people on the telephone. I make notes, then type 'em up. Cringe to think what my grandparents would make of a grown man spending his working life in such a manner. The life I have lived as a journalist, and that my cousins now live as doctors, lawyers, nurses, consultants, businesspeople, lab technicians, contractors, sports trainers, would have been unimaginable to my ancestors who lie in graveyards of such hamlets as Sydney Mines, Chester Basin and Windsor. For that matter, how high an opinion would Eva Mount—who died at the age of ninety-six— daughter of the late Angus and Catherine (Flynn) MacKeigan, have of such sedate people? The minister at her funeral told stories I'd heard many times before, but they now sounded fresh and exciting. About her days as secretary to J.B. McLaughlin, the fiery Scottish union leader who landed in Cape Breton just as the coal fields and steel plants were opening, when buying everything at the company store was a way of life and police rode down strikers in the streets of industrial Cape Breton. J.B., the people's hero, was reviled by the big capitalists and their toadies in government. When he was jailed on a trumped-up charge of seditious libel, it was Eva MacKeigan who delivered his food, along with news of the labour wars, to the Glace Bay jail, then smuggled out his speeches to be printed in local newspapers like the one where my grandfather Flash Demont worked.

"That's what you should be writing about," a cousin of my father's—whose children are known respectively as Old Foot, Big Foot, Red Foot and Little Foot—scolded as I left the reception after the funeral. And I had to agree. My past is my inheritance. There are the ancestors in whose lives I hope to find the secret of my own. There is the land where I seek to find the grown-over road behind to help me navigate the dimly lit path ahead.

I am the only member of my family not born in Cape Breton. So my first significant memory of the island involves a high-school basketball tournament and a night billeted on the floor of a Sydney high-school gym. Instead of sleep, a marathon two-on-two tournament that ended at 3:30 a.m. with a dislocated index finger. We were knocked out of the tournament early—slaughtered by a ratty-looking bunch from the neighbouring coal town of New Waterford who ran our legs off and played a game so different from ours that we might as well have been from different planets. I knew something was terribly amiss when their centre, a feared intimidator in big-city Halifax, threw an elbow at an opponent. Shoulder-length hair flying, the Cape Bretoner turned without missing a beat and tried to *drop kick* my teammate in the head. It was altogether the strangest thing I've ever witnessed on a basketball court.

Not that we cared. This was about being sixteen, on the road and finding yourself in this strange place where girls you've never seen before actually seemed to find you interesting. We made a nocturnal trip to the bootleggers in Whitney Pier, the home of Scottish, Jamaican and Italian steelworkers. Which was where I finally understood the meaning of an old exchange I'd been hearing for years between my parents: *Are you from the Bay, Boy?/No, I'm from the Pier, Dear.* Our hair was still wet from the shower as we ordered beers at a jovial little lounge on the edge of town. Then the day moved into evening like a slow dream. Only one image sticks clearly with me: watching the television and seeing Smokin' Joe Frazier being seized by panic and starting to run—truly a sad sight—with George Foreman in lumbering pursuit. After that it's all blurry and spinning around, the frigid rush of winter night air, a window breaking and a teammate trying to cart my suddenly paralyzed body across an icy field as the Mounties approach.

Prudently I pick this moment to fast-forward—I'm a parent now, for God's sakes—to the here-and-now, a summer day that begins with rain, then turns hazy and hot as I drive slowly through the Sydney streets. Sydney, it must be said, is not one of the great cities for sightseeing. To be frank, whole parts of it are seriously ugly. It does have a pretty little park with duck ponds to commend it; down around the harbour can be nice; the new office and shopping complex, the hotels and entertainment centre add an air of modernity. But head in the wrong direction, past the steel plant and the tar ponds, say, and you can drive for long without seeing a sight that lifts your heart. That is its legacy, the price it has always paid for its very existence. Looking at it dispassionately, some might say Sydney and the other towns of industrial Cape Breton appear an anachronism, without hope in this age of the information highway and the global economy.

I am looking today for the sad, drab building where I once lived. This was almost a decade after the indignity of the Riverview High tournament. I was then a newly minted university grad with my first job: sports reporter at the Cape Breton *Post*, a position I owed entirely to my father's cousin, Gordon "Moose" Mercer, king of a local mini-conglomerate who ate lunch every weekday with the paper's editor. Home was a windowless basement bachelor in a converted beauty salon. I survived on botched recipes from the *Joy of Cooking* and smoked meat sandwiches from Abe's Deli. My shift ran from 7 p.m. until 2 a.m. and consisted mainly of typing up slow-pitch softball scores. The challenges were not overwhelming: once I figured out the dozen different substitutions for the verb "to hit" (*crack, line, whistle, belt, smack, drive, hammer, wallop, clobber, rap, crucify* and, my personal favourite, *ding*). After I just threw up my hands and admitted that I never was going to get all the different MacDonalds, Rudderhams, MacNeils, MacKinnons and Abbasses right, things were pretty relaxing.

The newspaper office was full of quirks. So ancient looking and down at the heels that I imagine my grandfather would have felt at home. (A couple of old-timers in the composing room had actually worked with my grandfather at the *Gazette*.) The place smelled of vile vending machine coffee and industrial cleaner. When I arrived to punch in, a wire machine clucked away in the back room and a couple of stragglers from the day shift hammered at vintage Underwoods. Eccentrics and oddballs, I would later learn, walk all newsrooms, which are what we have instead of institutions.

Yet even by those loose standards the *Post* seemed special. Other staffers told me the real characters—the sports writer who pounded back rum-and-Coke all night, passed out on the typewriter keys, then arose with the alphabet imprinted on his forehead to rattle off the rest of his column—had moved on. An amazing thought for a rookie breathing the newsroom's musty rarefied air for the first time: the city editor looked and sounded as though he could put in a shift hauling slag at the steel plant without too much bother; the sports editor, who owned a bunch of harness racing trotters, had betting theories so elaborate they would make Stephen Hawking's head swim. A colleague in the sports department once turned on his tape recorder back in the newsroom. Instead of an interview with a journeyman NHLer on summer vacation we were treated to the unexpected sounds of he and a girlfriend in flagrante.

Yes, it was a fun place to be when everyone else was asleep as I tentatively tapped away on my first stories. Outside the newsroom, though, I was laughably out of sync with my surroundings. Trying to adapt to the unaccustomed shifts, I developed insomnia and often couldn't sleep until six in the morning. Since I was carless and really knew no one anyway, it got to the point where I'd wake at three in the afternoon and just stay in bed reading until it was time for another culinary surprise before the next shift. On my two nights off—one was Saturday evening, since the *Post* published no Sunday edition—I'd go to the racetrack or show up at the bar by the pizzeria and nurse a couple of beers by myself.

I never got my bearings. Running was a good example. Since then I've shuffled across the Rockies, lurched along the Grand Canal in Venice, stumbled through the hallucinogenic heat of Abilene, Tex. Sydney, though, was the ultimate adventure. One day, early in my stay, I cut through the Whitney Pier area. My joints and muscles felt nice and loose; I was breathing rhythmically. Everything was going fine until I happened by a house where a few guys about my age were drinking beer on the porch. "Hey, b'y, you're not from the Pier," one said as he bent down to pick up a rock the size of a loonie. Then all three of them were pegging stones at me as I high-tailed it down the road, looking over my shoulder like a stray dog someone had just put the run on.

The humiliations just seemed to keep coming. Couple of weeks later I was cooling down after my workout when a member of the Sydney constabulary appeared.

"Can I please see some identification," he said.

I was wearing a pair of green hospital orderly pants—then the rage as workout garb—which meant that all my pockets could hold was my apartment key. When I said I didn't have any his eyes narrowed into little slits.

"I just moved here," I said. "I work for the *Post*." I looked down at my greens—and it dawned on me. "Really. Honest. I'm not kidding. Call the paper. Go ahead, they'll vouch for me."

"Now just settle down, son," he said. Jesus, he thinks I'm going to run for it, he'll blackjack me or something, I'll wake up in a room with white walls, surrounded by people dressed like the Marx Brothers. . . .

Now it makes me lonesome to cruise by the *Post's* old home, where at noon every day the pensioners, pogey collectors and steelworkers on the night shift used to gather for the day's edition. Some time ago, Thompson Newspapers built it a shiny new head-quarters a couple of blocks away, which local chamber of commerce types hailed as the signal of the city's rebirth. A better symbol of Sydney, in my opinion, stands across the street, where a tavern that seemed old fifteen years ago lives on bedraggled as ever. For this is one of those towns where just surviving is victory enough.

Emigration, as usual, seems to be draining the area dry. And the threat that the subsidized steel plant and uncompetitive coal mines could evaporate hangs like factory smoke over Sydney and the surrounding towns. Yet there's a quiet endurance in the peo-ple that over centuries has helped them withstand the ravages of mine and plant closures, of company strike breakers, of famines, fires and cave-ins. In spite of the uncertainty, in spite of the dearth of prospects, in spite of having the highest rate of cancer in the country, in spite of living next to the infamous tar ponds—the mere mention of which drives environmentalists the country over into apoplexy—most people never really leave this poor, doomed, angry place. Sure, they move away. But those who do spend the rest of their lives as the banished, crowding into Caper Clubs in

Boston and Toronto desperate for any scrap of gossip about home.

"It's impossible to explain, eh," Rankin MacSween explained as we drove towards Whitney Pier one day. He's a lanky six-four, a bald, grey-bearded man with piercing eyes and a bass voice smooth as molasses. His is a familiar story. He grew up a few miles outside Sydney, headed for St. F.X. like all good Catholics from the island, then on to Ottawa to finish his criminology studies before starting a career with Corrections Canada. When his mother got sick he came back and never left. "I used to come over here when I was growing up and go to Fred Thomey's, this bar," he remembers. "There was never a set cover charge. You'd come in and he'd hold up five fingers, which meant five dollars, and you'd hold up two, kind of negotiating, see. Then he'd hold up three fingers and if you paid it, in you'd go. The bar was the same way. You'd order a beer and it would be a different price every night. It was a tough spot. There was a fight every couple of hours. There'd be knives and everything. It's a real wonder no one was ever killed."

Yes, he explains, there was a time when Whitney Pier was a thriving place and this street on which we are driving was full of businesses, stores and life. It's tough for everyone around here now; nobody has a sense that things are ever going to get any better. But the people of the Pier don't really care. "A real estate agent tells me that this is the strongest market anywhere in the area," MacSween adds. "Whenever a home comes up in the Pier someone is always ready to buy, because the people who grew up here always want to live here."

■ ■ ■

Cape Bretoners are not unique in this regard. Nova Scotians, no matter where they are from, believe in roots. They must, because so much about this place makes not a whit of sense in the economic view of things. Anybody can do well in Toronto, where a guy who isn't fit to cut bait down at the fishplant tools around in a four-wheel-drive and berates the Filipina nanny over the car phone. In fundamentally illogical places it takes real talent and cunning to survive. But they hold on anyway, because home does not come without a price and those lucky enough to find their place have to pass a test of faith in order to stay.

There is nothing downtrodden, in contrast, about Lunenburg. It is a rare place, with a harbour like a painting, a string of brightly coloured storefronts and block upon block of rambling, whimsical houses with widow's walks and oversized dormers built from a local design known as the Lunenburg bump. Beautiful enough that the United Nations recently designated it a world treasure. This is no museum, not yet anyway, even if the centuries of plundering the oceans, which always supported the area in high style, are finally drawing to a close. You just have to walk down the street to know that Lunenburg is never going to be some holiday spot for the idle rich like nearby Chester. Oh, sure, the people themselves are changing: more and more transplanted book publishers, authors and software designers who live here full-time, working by fax and modem and running up monster Fed Ex tabs. Someone in the county tax office told me that last year fourteen hundred tax bills from the area went to property owners back in Germany. But the independent flavour of the place comes from the locals—the descendants of the Protestant farmers from France, Switzerland and southwestern Germany. Tough kids raised to work on fishing boats aren't going to willingly stoop to being waiters or clerks. They aren't servants. Look one of them in the eye and you're staring at the genetic result of 250 years of being on your own, wondering if the next storm will destroy everything you own and when the fish will finally disappear.

These are people who for generations have travelled the sea lanes of the world on trawlers, frigates and cargo ships. Always they come home. In many ways Henry Demone, chief executive officer of National Sea Products, once the planet's biggest seafood company, and still Lunenburg's biggest employer, is typical. We're both French Huguenots, caucasian, roughly the same size and age. There the similarities end. While my clan seldom likes to step off terra firma, his father, Earl, started out as a hand on one of the last of Lunenburg's famed saltbank schooners and eventually became the captain of NatSea's imperious fishing fleet, once arguably the largest in the world. Henry wielded a mean filleting knife on the gutting line, where he worked summers in high school. After university he moved over to the corporate side at NatSea, then headed to France as the president of a French seafood importer and distributor. Eventually, he came back to run NatSea, which saw its glory days disappear along with the fish.

"One day Rena and I sat down and talked about it and realized that we didn't know anyone in either of our families who had ever married someone from outside of Lunenburg County," he mused over coffee one day. "It's kind of insular in that way here, I guess. But it makes for a strong Lunenburg County character. There's a strong work ethic here and a kind of privacy here. People do tend to resist change somewhat; we say that within our company. If you're trying to do something new it will probably happen quicker in the United States or Newfoundland. But in the end the people of Lunenburg County will probably do it as well if not better than the others."

At the crest of a hill on the outskirts of Sydney I turn back and look at a neatly trimmed graveyard above the dark satanic mills of the steel plant. Here, the scene seems to say, people live tough, bleak lives, die and are buried amongst their own in rocky soil that after generations of toil is theirs. But beyond, a stationary ferris wheel, the most visible piece of a travelling circus troupe, brightens the landscape. And I remember that irony is not unknown in these parts. Cape Bretoners, to steal a phrase I once saw used about the Spanish, are masters of the cosmic shrug. Like other people from hard places they take nothing short of mortality too seriously. They realize that life fundamentally is a cruel joke, but it is all that they have. So they tell stories.

Much is made of the place's isolated oral culture, how sitting around the kitchen table telling yarns instead of growing fat and stupid before the TV has enabled the traditions and old stories to stay alive. I believe it's as much because they find the whole thing so profoundly funny, in a black sort of way, that they just have to laugh. It is deeply therapeutic. Think of it as a glorious, profane celebration of existence. For out of these shared stories the pulse of life can be heard, like a drumbeat through time.

My brother and I grew up hearing stories about our family's island. We heard stories about cave-ins and colliery strikes, about the company store, owned by the British Empire Steel Corporation, which owned everything you ate and wore, even the house where you lived, about struggling to stay off the dole during the Depression years and about the cooperative movement, which my great-grandfather helped spawn so that the miners and their families could take a bit of control over their lives. We heard about magnificent athletes, of shell-shocked war veterans wandering the streets and the locals who left to make it big. We heard stories of murder, betrayal and just plain bad luck. We heard about the striking miners who built an effigy of my grandfather, complete with the long fur coat he used to wear as an inspector in the colliery and draped with an R.I.P. sign as a warning. We heard of the old country club behind the Sydney Mines police department where the English-born miners and their families met for a few pints and to sing the old dance-hall songs. We heard about the bootleg coal mines—essentially holes dug in people's cellars— and Freddy Lewis, the coal company cop who would peer into basements on the lookout for wrongdoing. About Murphys 49, the famous moonshine made out in Reserve Mines. About the semi-pro baseball players who roomed at my grandparents' home. And about Senator's Corner in Glace Bay, where Commercial St., Union St., Main St. and Upper Main St. all converged, where during the war years the townsfolk gathered to gossip each night and where every day my grandfather picked up his Boston *Post* and walked the six blocks home without lifting his head from the paper.

Charlie MacLeod's newsstand disappeared God knows when. But some of the other old landmarks at Senator's Corner live on: Ellie Marshall's Store, Markadnonis's Shoe Repair, the Savoy Theatre where the old R&B crooners the Platters, according to a poster now hanging in the window, are set to appear. Inside Senator's Gourmet Coffee I buy an oatcake and a cup of mocha java and ask a pleasant woman drinking iced tea if she knows anyone in my family. After a bit of back and forth we establish that my aunt Rea was her grade one teacher.

"The doctor DeMont?" she asks, referring to Rea's son, my cousin Bruce, who recently moved to a suburb of Chicago to open a medical practice. That end of my family, it seems to me, epitomizes the Cape Breton experience: one son forced to leave in his late thirties to take a job in the States; the other, Kenneth, a tough miner who lives where DeMonts for generations have lived.

"It's hard," she says with a resigned smile. "There's really no reason for young people to stay around here." She knows. Her son's CD is playing on the coffee shop sound system. But he is smart enough to be pursuing an engineering degree in Halifax in case the music career sputters. The point is made. Glace Bay, to the eye at least, seems on the verge of dissolution. Outside, the old-timer under the shady tree on Commercial St. looks forgotten, forlorn. The empty storefronts and the vacant lot where the United Church used to stand suggest the latter stages of decay.

Now I'm on more familiar turf—Knox Hall, where Grampie Flash once worked. Past the site of the old stone wall, now ripped down, where everyone used to sit at night when I visited as a teen. Then up York St. towards the house where my father grew up. I'm working by memory, with no actual address to go by. All I have are images: a screened-in front porch; the kitchen, rich with baking smells, where most of the life in the house occurred; the backyard, where my father and his brothers Eric and Earl buried swordfish bills so that the insects would pick them clean to make weapons for their games of Robin Hood and the knights of the Round Table.

I look hard from across the road, but find nothing familiar. It's depressing to stand on a hot airless street recognizing not a thing, feeling rootless and lonely. It occurs to me that this must be what it is like to have Alzheimer's disease. I walk back to my car, start it up and begin scanning for a sign back to the highway. A couple of turns and I'm at a stoplight. A car full of teenage girls pulls up beside me. They're singing some pretty old song that's more my generation than theirs. When I look towards them they howl with laughter, then tear off, leaving the notes trailing behind. I can't quite place the title. But it's the voices that hold me there after the light has turned. I know them from somewhere. I'm sure of it.

Thirteen

Home Is
Where the Heart Is

AND NOW FOR THE DOWNSIDE. IT CAN BE A TERRIBLE BURDEN, THIS ENDLESS search for place, connection and belonging. The quest can transform a person into something haunted and driven, a member of some lost tribe, the Flying Dutchman, the Ancient Mariner. But maybe finding that special place—then losing it—is the worst thing. Then you become an exile with a far-away stare, wandering dazedly through places you don't want to be, searching for something that reminds you of home. I know because I've walked in their sad footsteps. Whenever I used to tell someone that my favourite place in the world is Nova Scotia, they would tilt their head and look at me like a terrier hearing one of those whistles with a pitch too high for human ears. They knew they were in for it now—a long, meandering treatise about the smell of the sea, the spirit of the people etc. etc. that would get so vague and hard to follow that soon even my own head would be spinning. The whole time they'd be waiting, hoping I would at least slow down enough that they could politely make an excuse and slip away. But I would just keep going, laying down my homesick rap, while the room emptied around me.

Cottages were another thing. Our family had never owned one. But I loved the theory of them. Houses would come and go. A cottage, though, was timeless—that place where you and your kids and grandkids could always return to and find it the same in 2006 as in 1956. While I lived contentedly in apartments in Toronto, my desire for home manifested itself in this weird need to own a recreational property. Not a ski chalet in Whistler or an over-priced shack up in the Muskokas. No, I wanted something on the freezing Atlantic Ocean. Two days' solid drive away.

Lisa, a much wiser and more practical person, even bought in to this strange obsession. I'd pick up Saturday editions of the Halifax *Chronicle-Herald* at the local newsstand, then spend a good hour or so poring over the real estate ads, peppering her with stupid questions about square footage, oceanfrontage versus waterfrontage and what perc-tested meant. Next, phone calls to agents on the South Shore, the Northumberland Strait and Cape Breton where I'd make like a high-roller from Hogtown, asking how far it was from this place or that to the nearest airport, where I implied I would be parking the private jet. I was convincing enough to at least get on their mailing lists. Which meant that every few weeks a brochure, enticing as pornography, would come sliding in the mail slot advertising something like "Near Peggy's Cove 36 minutes from Halifax, desirable seafront property, house on deep, saltwater inlet. Boathouse, private wharf, large garden. Property includes 3+ undeveloped acres with lake frontage." Then a long, elaborate fantasy about how we might finance such a purchase.

Somewhere, deep in my heart, we had to know this whole cottage thing was a non-starter. But all the time we were living away we persisted. To the point that during vacations we'd actually take an occasional afternoon and go "cottage hunting." Nothing scientific—just drive around little out-of-the-way places looking for For Sale signs. If we saw one down some lonely stretch of road, we'd pull over and actually spend a few minutes wandering around the property. We'd peer in windows, pace off the lot for size, talk to a few neighbours. Eventually we'd jot down the agent's number, one of us would say, "I'm gonna call them tomorrow," and we'd drive off. We always managed to find a reason not to make that call.

It made no sense, but what does in life? You travel, stay put, move on, settle, go, die. It is all beyond your control. You want to go home, but work, love or something else stands in the way—and you find the trail grown over, the highway moved, the way back lost. You feel the need to put past and family behind you, then discover you cannot because they are in the way you walk, the cells of your skin, your twisted neuroses and your shining virtues.

Home, however you define it, is all about longing and loss, loyalty and conflict. The search turns us into mad zealots, mumbling as we stumble down blind alleys. We become like Rev. Norman McLeod, the charismatic clergyman who led a boatload of Scottish followers to Pictou in the early nineteenth century at the peak of the Highland migration. He was a bit of a nut—a moral dictator who imposed severe punishments for trivial "sins." He found this frozen, demanding place was not the promised land of his visionary dreams. When a letter came from Highlanders who had settled in the Ohio Valley inviting him to be their minister he accepted the call. McLeod left by ship, a bunch of his followers in tow, but hardly got through the Strait of Canso before their vessel was driven back up the coast of Cape Breton. They gave up and settled in the harbour of St. Anns. Yet it still wasn't right. The old dream reawakened nearly thirty years later when he received a letter from a relative singing the praises of Australia. McLeod was a fierce-eyed old man by then. He boarded a boat with 135 of his parishioners and headed for Australia, which also proved disappointing, and they eventually settled in the New Zealand colony of Waipu. From there they sent back wonderful reports of this new land. Soon another nine hundred people from St. Anns built ships and joined them. They live still in the place where the old man stopped wandering, the search over. Finally.

That's home. It attracts and repels, haunts you when you're not even there, then breaks your heart when you return. You can have this series of connected thoughts anywhere. In a lumber camp in British Columbia, a dank, cool tavern in Boston. One day I was on the Isle of Skye, in the Scottish Hebrides, sipping on a big pint of beer outside a pub that was so close to the road that I had to lean backwards to avoid getting pulverized when the occasional truck or car came along. I was half listening to the conversation inside when I heard the words "Cape Breton." I walked in, took a few seconds to adjust my eyes to the dimness and beheld this bearded giant in a thick sweater, shorts and hiking boots who looked ready to fight the Battle of Culloden all over again. Within minutes he was telling me his story: how he was born here seventy-odd years ago, the son of an opera singer who lost his voice. Then moved to Halifax when his father secured a teaching post at the old conservatory and grew up on the street where we now lived. His was a nomadic, unsettled life. He ended up living in the Sierra Mountains of California. Now he was thinking about moving back to Skye, near his people. "I can't explain it," he said after raising his glass in the direction of a wrinkled-faced elder who sat regally across the scarred oak bar. "It may be the wrong thing to do. But it just feels right."

I've felt the same way too many times to recount. Like everyone I felt an urge to cast off the shackles of home, even if the shackles were largely self-imposed. The push and pull mean the soul and emotions are forever in conflict. Sometimes it is easier to see this in others than in ourselves, which is why one day I found myself in the vivid little hamlet of Blue Rocks just outside Lunenburg. I first heard of the place from a doorman at the Halifax newspaper where I worked. He possessed a great wreck of a face—all broad planes and huge gloomy features as expressive as an Easter Island statue. Chugging purposefully towards Blue Rocks for the first time, I discover he looked just like the little village where he was born.

I'm trying to imagine how the village might have looked nearly seventy years ago. The road was probably rutted dirt rather than blacktop. But the boulder-strewn landscape, the churches, square wooden homes, weathered fish houses and wharfs seemed time-less. I have no idea if the two men I have in mind ever laid eyes on each other. But if they did, it could have happened at the end of a ramshackle wharf where the fishing buoys are stacked like toys.

Art, no matter how you define it, bubbles from some pretty unlikely wellsprings. But I still find it truly wonderful that at the same moment as Marsden Hartley, one of the great painters of the twentieth century, was locked away painting his solemn land-scapes, he could have stuck his head out of his studio window and heard this noise—to his ears perhaps not even quite human—which would have been the first tentative yodels of Hank Snow, on his way to becoming the singing ranger of the Grand Ole Opry.

Maybe the two never did speak. But here in this unlikely place—in the strangest of juxtapositions—their life-lines briefly crossed. Not in some fleeting way, though. Blue Rocks, for one, meant inno-cent, unrestrained love and a sense of home that had always elud-ed Snow. For the other life on the South Shore was a deep wound that scabbed over but never totally healed.

By the time he arrived in Lunenburg, Hartley was sick, beaten-down and, at fifty-eight, old beyond his years. He was coming off a miserable winter in New York, living on sixty cents a day and one decent meal a week, which his dealer, Alfred Stieglitz, bought for him. So down and out was he that he had to destroy more than a hundred paintings and drawings because he couldn't afford to rent a storage vault. Somehow he scraped together enough money to head for Bermuda, where he spent several months recuperating and painting a series of tropical-fish fantasies. He decided against returning to Gloucester, Mass., the picturesque fishing village where he spent most summers, because he disliked its "summer art colony" set and because it was too expensive. Then he remembered his friend Frank Davison—a novelist who wrote under the pseudonym Pierre Coalfleet—and how he often talked about his hometown of Lunenburg. When he arrived he missed his friend by a single day. Hartley found Lunenburg dull, its citizens gauche. Taking the advice of a taxi driver, he went up the coast four miles to Blue Rocks. There he found the Masons. And much more.

Hartley was a wanderer. He was born in Lewiston, Me., in 1877, and had just turned eight when his mother died. Three years later his father remarried, moved to Cleveland and left the son with a married sister. "From the moment of my mother's death," he wrote, "I became in psychology an orphan, in consciousness a lone thing left to make its way out for all time after that by itself." Thus the quest began. He was searching for something, perhaps seeking an idealized version of Maine, the birthplace where he could no longer live because of the painful memories there. So he studied in Cleveland and New York, returned to Maine to paint its flat mountains and at twenty-two mounted his first one-man New York show. In later years he lived in Berlin and Munich, spent time in New Mexico, lectured on Dada in Paris and painted in a Cézanne-like manner in Aix-en-Provence, never living longer than ten months in a single house. Hartley found temporary solace from the burning loss of his father in the arms of a series of young

German army officers in decadent pre–World War One Berlin. But that comfort evaporated when one of his particular favourites died in the early days of the conflict.

Then he found the tiny island of Eastern Points by Blue Rocks, where the strangest thing happened. "I fell in love with the most amazing family of men & women the like of which I have never in my life seen," he wrote to a friend after meeting the Masons, a fishing clan who had lived there for generations. Nothing figurative—he seemed to have meant love of the head-over-heels, pain-in-the-solar-plexus variety. Francis and Martha, the parents, "are so utterly & completely free of neuroses of any sort, and maintain an enviable balance between the material & the spiritual worlds that they symbolize for me the term, ideal," he gushed. Their two sons drove him to even more embarrassing rapture. "I love both Alty & Donny & if I were a woman I'd have a time choosing," he wrote, "for Alty is wild and all flair, all demonstrative. Donny is shy as a thrush and never ventures out of the deep forests of his being until he is sure that he is safe." Just think about it for a second: this dissipated world-weary sophisticate, friend and confidant of Mabel Dodge, John Reid, Hart Crane and Gertrude Stein searching the world for something to love and finding it amongst these wild, noble folk on the South Shore with their beauty, spirituality, endurance and loathing of cheap affectation. "I feel as if I had found my chosen people," he said in a letter to a friend back in America. "Think of me being completely happy in the arms of the Mason family."

This was one smitten man. He boarded with the Masons for a

month, returned to New York for a show that was savaged by the critics, then headed back to Eastern Points. It was a tranquil, productive summer. He finished the last in a series of paintings begun in Gloucester, this time using the boulder-strewn landscape of Blue Rocks as a model. Evenings were quiet affairs, often spent listening to the radio in the Mason family parlour. He bragged about how he was becoming a good seaman from spending time on fishing boats and mused about building a shack near the family.

Then, the calm shattered. "I don't want to tell you what I have to tell," he wrote to a friend, "but a terrible tragedy has fallen on our home here, & the two big lovely boys of the family & their pretty young cousin were drown Saturday night in the teeth of the gale that swept up from Florida all along the Atlantic seaboard." Wracked with anguish, Hartley wanted to leave, but one of the daughters persuaded him to say to provide support for the ageing parents. In despair, he closeted himself away in the boys' old blacksmith shop, painting his brooding landscape scenes and working on a manuscript called *Cleophas and His Own*. Eventually he returned to New York. Years later he began a series of paintings based on the Masons, the first figurative works of his career, which he called a commemoration of "one of the most elevating experiences of my life—in truth the most elevating." Finally he moved back to Maine, where he died of heart failure.

Yale got hold of the first draft of *Cleophas*. The original subtitle was "A North Atlantic Episode." The word *Episode* has been crossed out and replaced with *Tragedy*. In the text he writes:

I went to the cemetery before I left, I told no one, I didn't want anyone around—the seagulls swirled over my head, the breeze blew furtively around my body, the white fence showed where their estate began and ended, I looked down into the earth as far as I could and I said, only the seagulls hearing—"Adelard and Etienne, I loved you more than myself, I love you because I was equal with you in every way but the strength, and it was the strength that fortified me—I truly loved you."

I did not wait for plausible replies, I could only hear the wind rustling among the paper flowers, twisting the worn petals east to west.

I came to the yarn in a round-about way after I read about how a fraudulent Toronto stockbroker had spent $200,000 for a Nova Scotia landscape of Hartley's entitled *Church on the Moors* and wondered why I'd never heard of the painter. Today I find not a hint of his life around Blue Rocks. I do get a glimpse of what I think was the house where the old painter would have cast those amorous glances at the young fishermen. But I'm a little reluctant to go around asking members of the Mason clan about the whole business. For all I know the event could stand as some seminal event in family history. If I asked a Mason about something that happened at some particular moment in time, she might reply, "Well, let's see, it was fifty-five years, seven months, four days and eleven hours after that painter fella fell in love with Alty and Donny," then shake her head.

Hartley? Everything I know about him indicates that brief period may have been *the* moment. No matter what came after—no matter how deep into despair he would sink—he would always have Blue Rocks, the Masons and the perfection they symbolized. It was something he carried with him always, like a fetish.

For Hank Snow, Nova Scotia was something altogether different. He is in his eighties now, a frail little man living in Nashville whose voice can no longer stand the strain of the hard-driving songs that are his trademark. On the South Shore of Nova Scotia, where he hails from, no one seems to remember his rough, uneducated ways, his drinking, his brawling and his monster ego. Or maybe they just love him all the more *because* of the nightmare side of the Hank Snow saga. Either way, Brooklyn has its Hank Snow Park and Liverpool the Hank Snow Country Music Centre, complete with photos of the fishing schooners he worked on, his cream 1947 Cadillac convertible, a 1928 T. Eaton Special guitar like the one he owned and a collection of Fuller brushes similar to the ones he peddled around Halifax when times were tough.

In my view the best shrine to his life and career is in Blue Rocks, at Graham "Buz" Baker's house, which is perched atop a little hill across the road from the water. Baker is a rough-hewn Renaissance man, a seascape painter, fierce Red Sox fan and Lunenburg's harbour master. He is also an articulate expert on the history of country-and-western music. If anyone acts as the keeper of Hank Snow's flame around here it is this tall, raw-boned, slightly dangerous looking red-head. Throw a Stetson on him—which is what he wears when he's fronting his country blues combo—and he's the mirror of one of those hungry-looking Steinbeck cowboys who showed up on the stage of the Opry the same time as Snow. Like his hero and hundreds of other Maritimers, Baker grew up in the sway of the hillbilly music of the rural South, which he heard camped in front of the radio listening to nighttime broadcasts from the Allegheny Mountains. "I think the hard times we've always experienced in the Maritimes breeds an interest in country music," he says when I ask why Snow, Wilf Carter and so many other top-notch old-time C&W talents emerged from these hard-scrabble shores. "When people don't have the money to go out and do anything else they have to entertain themselves. I'm firmly convinced that coming from here led to the blossoming of these talents. Country music is the music of the people who work close to the earth, the fishermen, the farmers, the lumberjacks, the miners, all of whom had difficult lives. Country music is just the blues with a twang."

And Clarence Eugene Snow was born to the blues. He came into this world in a tiny house in Brooklyn, a milltown sixty miles west of Blue Rocks, in 1914, the fifth of six children born to George Lewis Snow and Marie Alice Boutilier. For some reason his school-mates started calling him Jack. The name stuck until he began recording in 1936. By that point, he knew first-hand about struggle, misery, disappointment and the other standbys of the country songwriter's stable. His parents had split when he was six and he became the responsibility of an abusive grandmother who forbade him to see his mother and had him put in jail when he rebelled. By the time mother and son were reunited she had hooked up with a sociopathic fisherman who liked nothing better than to bounce the youngster off the four walls of their decrepit house.

To escape the abuse he got a job on a Grand Banks schooner sailing out of Lunenburg. He was twelve at the time, small for his age and fragile at that. But he stuck it out for four years, enduring the storms and the backbreaking work, marvelling at the sharks that followed their ship and the icebergs that seemed as high as mountains. At sea he often entertained the crew by playing the mouth organ, doing a sort of tap dance he'd made up and singing songs he had learned from his mother, including "Was There Ever a Pal Like You" and "The Wreck of the Altoona," which he heard on the family Victrola. When the crew really liked the performance they'd give him pieces of homemade fudge and throw him the occasional nickel. He spent the $5.95 earned from his first voyage on a guitar through the Eaton's mail-order catalogue.

Back on dry land he hustled like everyone else to cobble together a living in the Depression, trying bootlegging and diving off the wharf at Blue Rocks for nickels and dimes thrown by tourists. Once he nearly cut off his hand while splitting kindling wood and had to walk four miles in the dark to see a doctor in Lunenburg. But he was young and ambitious, dreaming of the big time, a full belly and fame. His first musical gig was a minstrel show in Bridgewater, which he performed in blackface. He was nineteen, wearing his best suit of clothes and lugging his guitar (now upgraded to a $12.95 model) when he bluffed his way into the offices of CHNS Radio in Halifax. After hearing him play, the station's chief engineer asked him to come back that night at seven to do a live fifteen-minute show. When the station offered him a Saturday-night spot he decided to change his stage name to Hank Snow the Yodeling Ranger after his idol Jimmie Rodgers. Soon he was spending his mornings trying to sell Fuller brushes in the slums of Halifax before heading to the radio station for a noon-hour spot as part of a combo set up to raise the profile of a company that sold a potion with "laxative qualities."

The Gaiety Theatre in downtown Halifax offered him a three-day job performing solo before an afternoon kids' matinee. I love the image of him showing up the first day, wearing a white satin shirt his mother made with full sleeves, a big wide collar with a red star on each tip and another big red star on each breast. The shirt had black silk laces that ran up the front just like the shirts Gene Autry, the singing cowboy, wore in the movies. Snow added black dungarees with a white cotton strip sewn down each leg and an orange and red neckerchief. On New Year's Eve he was scheduled to appear at the exclusive new Capitol Theatre. The manager took one look at his outfit and ordered him to change into an usher's uniform before he could step on stage.

In 1936 he signed with RCA Victor and made his first records. Back in the Maritimes he started to develop a following in places like Lockeport, Shelburne, Riverport, Hubbards Cove, Chester,

Sherbrooke and Ecum Secum, where he toured with his band throughout the 1940s playing in church halls, Legions, movie theatres and garages. He added a trio of black entertainers who tap-danced and did a comedy routine. Then he got hooked on the idea of making it in the States, moving to Wheeling, W. Va., where he bought a trained horse named Shawneee, outfitted him with an expensive silver saddle and began a travelling road show. Finally he landed a job on the Grand Ole Opry. Even that didn't help his sad little career. When Snow happened in 1950 to mention to an Opry official that he was thinking of buying a house, he was urged to hold off. In truth, Snow was on the verge of getting fired when a 45 he had written and recorded, *I'm Moving On,* took off like crazy, going number one on *Billboard* magazine's charts for an unprecedented forty-nine straight weeks. Hank Snow had finally arrived.

"He did have talent," Baker says, walking me through his collection of the Great Man's memorabilia: the covers of the albums spanning the thousand-or-so songs he recorded, photos of him being inducted into the Country Music Hall of Fame and the Songwriters Hall of Fame and performing at the Hollywood Bowl and the London Palladium. "But you have to remember that he is a Taurus. He has this tenacious perseverance to see something through to the end. And that is what really carried him through difficult times. And I mean he did have difficult times. Out of school when he was in grade five, a broken family, and I've even heard him say on stage that he carries the marks on his body from the beatings by his stepfather. Times were tough and here he is in this backwater of a place trying to make a name for himself as the Singing Cowboy. And I think that if he hadn't known such hard times he would not have been able to sing with such passion about it."

I take his point. Nova Scotia left Snow one hurt, wounded man; how could it have done otherwise? Even someone as untutored in country-western music as I am realizes you've got to live all those things—all the pain, poverty and loneliness—to sing songs that resonate like Snow's. Whether the price was worth it only he can say. He had no choice, of course. You can't escape who you are; you can't escape the place you call home; all you can do is make your peace with it.

Fourteen

Tales from the Fog City Diner

———

OUR HOUSE IN HALIFAX IS A LITTLE LIKE A TIME CAPSULE. WHEN I LOOK OUT our living-room window I can see the classroom where I attended grade one and the steps where, when I was extra-good, the teacher let me clean the chalkboard erasers after school. Sometimes I'll see the sister of the guy who that same year used a baseball bat to provide the rakishly handsome scar I bear over my left eyebrow. Sometimes standing on our back deck, performing the timeless male ritual of charring red meat over open flame, I see one of my oldest friends walking his dog on the field where we both shivered in the dark as kids sipping our first beer. Once, as I was coming out the front door, I was greeted with the wonderful sight of my old Cub leader, now in his late seventies at least, screaming down the street at the wheel of a motor scooter.

Normally I am not one to dwell too long on the past. It can be a paralyzing thing to meet one's history at every corner, in every closet and cupboard. Sometimes the best thing to do is just face it head on. One day in the grip of an unusual nostalgic reverie, I asked the phys-ed teacher at my old high school, which is just blocks from our house, whether I could visit the locker-room where I once dressed as a weak-shooting guard on the Queen Elizabeth Lions "A" basketball team. I discover the interior still looks like a Jackson Pollock painting—fifty years of names layered over each other to form this psychedelic pastiche of colours. Man, I wasted a lot of time down here when I should have been in class memorizing the kings of England, conjugating French verbs and cutting up crayfish. Yes, I would be a better, brighter, more stable person today if I had never discovered this dungeon; we all would be. I have to look hard amongst the names on the walls, but find some from my years: football players who became television actors or reborn Christians, hockey players who sell cars or were shot dead in drug feuds, basketball stars who work in the dockyard or drive blue Mercedes sedans with leather interiors.

I slip into the halls of the school, which take on the soft-lens quality of a movie dream sequence, all the time waiting for the background music to swell. Summer vacation, so the place is empty. All the better to imagine the sorry figure I cut back then, clomping around in my construction boots, even though I had never done anything remotely resembling labour, and sporting jeans wide enough to blot out the sun. No doubt I will burn in eternal hell for wearing a leisure suit to my grade twelve graduation ceremony. We spent a lot of time in cars—just friggin' around, heading for a gym to play basketball, to the Sahara for pizza and to the movies. On summer weekends we drove down the loopy stretch of highway for Queensland Beach. We'd use fake IDs to sneak into the South Gate (now an office tower) or the Lighthouse (now a peeler bar, but still called the Lighthouse). Sometimes we'd just drive aimlessly through the streets with the windows down, the radio turned up full, pretending the dash was a keyboard. Everyone doing the Billy Preston cross-over move, crooning "Come on world/join in/come love/love train" as if those were actually the words.

Nostalgia is a truly dangerous thing. Going home to recapture your lost youth can only end badly—even in a place like Halifax, which to the eye has not changed appreciably in a long, long time. But of course it has. And thank God for that, since so much of what you so fondly remember was simply being a kid with life and the world out there ahead of you. With the wisdom of age I can now appreciate that when I grew up here Halifax's energy lay buried, sunk beneath a provincial regard for authority and a misty-eyed longing for bygone days. This was the kind of place where you could never escape your past. Where growing up white and Protestant in the South End meant a good frat at Dal, an overpriced cottage on the South Shore and an early partnership at one of the old law firms. Once this had to be one of the most homogeneous cities on the continent.

Now look at it. Sometime between when I left and returned everyone under the age of twenty-five seems to have landed in Halifax. Along with the youth, the place has a more cosmopolitan look and feel: growing numbers of eastern Europeans and Asians stroll about; Birkenstock-shod baby boomers, here for the lifestyle, push carriages; young blacks and whites mix freely; female lovers walk arm in arm; no one bats an eye at the middle-aged man wearing the pumps and the nice conservative blue dress. The city still has the appearance of being stodgy and staid at the top: the same old canny Irish pols running city hall and the same well-fed lawyers running the provincial government. But that's all very deceiving, really. Halifax, for the first time in my life, has real sizzle. Something more is going on here than an influx of yuppies who know the difference between Java the computer language and a caffè latte. There's a sense of breathless liberation out there, the type that can only come from years of pent-up repression and slavish obedience to convention.

Inside a coffee shop, say. Not one of the trendy new ones where the technonerds bash away on laptops over double cappuccinos. But in Perks, sandwiched between the ferry terminal and the city's law courts, where on any weekday the self-styled "waterfront intelligentsia" are well into their usual groove. Halifax, technically, is a city, the fourteenth largest one in the country by last count. But spiritually it is a small town, full of places like this: bars, coffee shops and greasy-spoon diners where the clientele is fixed and the talk a loose banter based on an intimate knowledge of everyone else's business. I'm a virtual stranger here. But even I sense things falling into their practised rhythm: the stockbroker and Tory bagman arguing golf clubs with a corporate lawyer; the president of the provincial Liberal party who stops by to pick up a paper and trade political gossip. Yet look over there—at the blues-loving Italian-Canadian judge with the Al Pacino beard and haircut, at the writer freshly returned from Vancouver to work for one of the burgeoning film production houses ordering her morning hit, at the music promoter in the midst of putting together a summer comedy festival for the thousands of tourists who flock to the city to see what the buzz is about.

I know what you're saying. What about the depressed, downtrodden blacks who still wallow in poverty and hopelessness? What about the paucity of women holding political power, partnerships at the big law firms and high-level executive jobs? The only way I can respond is to say that you had to grow up here, like I did, go away to give yourself a little distance, then come back. To say Halifax is emerging from the Dark Ages is too severe. So let's just say that somewhere along the line the conservative capital of Nova Scotia rediscovered a lost youth to go with its penetrating sense of history. Maybe you can't go home again—if home means the exact place you left behind. Because both you and it have inevitably changed. So don't even bother looking. Just look at the place fresh as if for the first time. Consider it on its own merits; draw your own conclusions.

Opening my eyes wide I found Halifax now had charm, eccentricity and style along with a salty past. At some point the city went from being this colonial outpost port on the edge of the continent to the kind of place the rest of North America, whether it realizes it or not, fantasizes about being. I roll the words around my tongue, almost in disbelief: *Halifax the hip*. And what I wonder, staring out at the waterline through the coffeeshop window, is how did it happen?

■ ■ ■

Daybreak is the time down here. When the morning fog still cools the air and no one else is around down on the waterfront. Then, as the mist clears, and the outlines of the harbour emerge as in a Polaroid snapshot, I like to picture the scurvy-ridden British pioneers arriving, the booty-laden privateer ships that plundered all the way down the eastern seaboard coming to dock, and the Second World War convoys massing before leaving for Europe. I sometimes like to come down in the early morning and stare into the same green waters as the admirals who once plotted Britain's campaign to hold on to the New World. From here I can see the spot where a German submarine torpedoed a Canadian minesweeper and the place where the French steamship *Mont Blanc* and the Belgian steamer *Imo* collided, causing the biggest manmade explosion the world had seen until the horrors of Hiroshima. I can see the spot where the Pony Express news packet from Europe was dropped over the side of a Cunard steamer onto a boat at the harbour entrance and then passed to a rider on shore who galloped through town towards Digby. I can throw a rock to the beach where the makeshift gallows once stood, the bodies dangling in the air as a warning to all who entered the great, long harbour.

Halifax is a long time coming. There is nothing flimsy about it. Wander around awhile and you have a sense that it is firmly planted on the ground, that its wooden homes and brick buildings can withstand anything the North Atlantic can throw at it. It is built to last. Here, in a place with 250 years of rollicking, myth-laden life, the past so overlays the present that history is vibrant and alive. You get the sense that it comes from a tradition, a sense that begins with the name—stodgy, upright, just reeking of Empire—but is just as evident in Government House, the Lieutenant Governor's residence, and the other old buildings, now occupied by the people and preoccupations of the present, but where I'm certain the ghosts of the past still lurk.

Once it was reputed to be the wickedest town in North America, full of whorehouses, waterfront blind pigs, marauding press gangs, duels, drinking bouts and gambling dens. A murder ten years after the Red Coats arrived illustrates the wide-open frontier feel to the place: three gentlemen, Lieutenant Collins, Captain Sweeney and Dr. Johns, spent the night boozing at the house of one John Field and then went in search of whores up on Barracks St. Johns and Sweeney testified that they knocked at a door and "inquired for Polly." But since they were pounding on the wrong door, Polly was unavailable. When, according to one chronicler, "they waxed strong over this flouting of their legitimate desires and diversions the householder, one Lathum, discharged a musket and killed Lieutenant Collins. Captain Sweeney promptly called the town guard and the spirited Lathum, a baker, was tried and hanged."

The hangman at the time was probably a character known as Tomahawk who lived in a lonely hut at the city's farthest North End. He was a busy man, since in those days a person could be strung up for stealing a sheep or anything else worth four shillings.

Say this for Tomahawk, though, he had a heart; he hated his work so much that he drank himself to death trying to dull the pain. And here's a story that will warm your heart: some young lads discovered his body. Instead of calling the undertaker, they threw a noose around his neck and dragged it across the street to the ruin of a blockhouse. There they pitched what was left of old Tomahawk into the latrine. For years his bones lay there, a persistent attraction for the curious townspeople who often came for a peek at the remains.

It was always a small place destined to be part of big news, as either a bit player or a central participant. "Every handful of earth here has crumbled history," bluenose novelist Thomas Raddall once said about the city. Wolfe and the British brass feasted at the Great Pontac Hotel, emptying twenty-five bottles of brandy, fifty of claret and seventy of Madeira before setting sail for that rendezvous on the Plains of Abraham that ended French power in North America. Prince Edward turned it into the strongest fortress in North America during the Napoleonic Wars. During the War of 1812 Halifax was the centre of Britain's North American military power.

Everyone seems to have passed across this canvas. Two prime ministers and two fathers of Confederation are buried here. So are the bodies of 190 of the *Titanic*'s drowned men, women and children. Leon Trotsky, bound for the Russian Revolution, was jailed here. A quiet young lieutenant in the Royal Navy, William Edward Parry, dreamed of the Northwest Passage here. I like to picture it in the post-Waterloo days when young Joe Howe, the father of responsible government, was playing ball in the streets. Thomas Haliburton, Sam Slick's creator, had just been admitted to the Nova Scotia bar. James Gordon Bennett, the founder of the New York *Herald,* was teaching school. Samuel Cunard, still years away from starting his shipping line, was a rising young merchant. Abraham Gesner, the discoverer of kerosene, was trying to make up his mind whether to be a surgeon or a geologist.

But after the Second World War and the V-E Day Riots that left the city ruined and baffled, something snapped. A layer of Puritan repression blanketed the place, leaving it stagnant, depressed and dull, a dying port and garrison town holding on to its storied past. The city did have a brief moment in the sun when, during the late 1960s, draft dodgers and visiting actors and artists spread the word in the United States about an easygoing "San Francisco North" in Nova Scotia. Back then, the Nova Scotia College of Art and Design—hailed by *Art in America* as possibly "the best art school in North America"—exerted an influence throughout the continental art world that defied its small size and out-of-the-way location. All the same, by the 1980s the city's fizz had definitely gone flat.

Which brings us to now. Make no mistake: Halifax's spirit is still fundamentally logical and realist, as befits a city of government, universities and the military. But the city is in flux more than usual now, and out of that flux some strange things are sprouting. It is not a flashy city, a city that shouts "Look at me!" You have to be alert. When the sun breaks through, softening the hard edges of the Victorian and Georgian buildings and glimmering off the water, the city shimmers like a fairy tale. Me, I have always preferred Halifax's veiled seductions—the half-concealed, the shadowy, the illusion that something else is at work, something you cannot really comprehend. On nights on the waterfront when only the massive bases of the piers, grain elevators and spiffy new office towers show under the fog, a sense of gravity, melancholy and romantic mystery clings to the city.

Secret subcultures thrive all over. Even for someone like me who has spent most of his life here, strange things approach from all directions. Once, for example, I walked over to the elegant old Via Rail station, now a shadow of its former bustling self, and up some elegant stairs. There I found hallways full of small businesses—tailors, dry-goods suppliers, footwear dealers, this secret commercial world where tough no-nonsense men who looked like they never saw sunlight made a living servicing the ships and sailors who docked nearby. Another day I drove up a ramp into a derelict pier just down the way and found a flock of painters and sculptors at work high above the harbour. Who'd have thought? Just like who would have thought that the kick-boxing club down the road became a speakeasy when the bars closed, where it was possible to drink an absurdly over-priced rum-and-Coke standing inside the square ring, even bury a couple of hooks into the heavy bag if the mood suited. Across town, inside an old warehouse a friend owns in the city's hard-nosed North End, a couple of dozen alternative bands simultaneously try to blow the doors off their sound-proof bunkers each night. Farther downtown, the digital revolution is in full swing in a forgotten office building, even though a whole squad of local technowizards who used to work their magic there were carried off to Seattle on a recent Bill Gates hiring binge. Closer to home, I once stopped into a coffee shop carrying Sam in a backpack and gaped at a dozen or so wild-haired Amazons spinning across the floor in some high-spirited, exotic dance resembling nothing I'd seen before.

Nothing should surprise me any more. You want characters? What about the tiny old man with the mass of snow-white hair—an Austrian maestro who rides his bicycle through the streets twelve months of the year? What about the university president and classicist who still occasionally likes to get out in a lobster boat where he used to earn a decent living? What about the pair of ex-pat Brits who publish *Frank,* the scandal sheet, which no one admits to reading even though *everyone* seems familiar with the contents of each ratty-looking issue? What about the older woman I see every day outside my house, dwarfed by the white Cadillac she drives ever so slowly beside her short-haired terrier, which is on the sidewalk taking its daily walk?

Booze cans, bootleggers, oddballs—I don't want to give you the wrong impression. One after another the nasty old fictions that made up the city's lore—the wet-blanket puritanism, the religious, social and racial divisions, the old-style politics—are being tossed aside. What remains, by and large, is the good stuff that has always made the place different.

That and how it feels so cool to be in Halifax now.

■ ■ ■

Night in the city now. My brother-in-law John and his girlfriend, Jenny, have agreed to act as guides. Their Halifax has cardinal points. Right now we are descending some beat-off stairs redolent of sour spilt beer into a place I once knew as the Ladies Beverage Room, now magically transformed into a hip little spot called the Oasis. In my memory underage high-school kids and university students drink quarts, drug dealers do a stiff trade in the corner, downtown professionals who just hadn't made it home from the office yet order another round. Or am I just feeling a shade out of touch as I stand waiting for the band to rev up its instruments, listening to the click-click-click of the pool balls. I shoot some mediocre stick, down a couple of big glasses of Moosehead. I scan the crowd for faces that look remotely like mine. The only people who appear as out of place as I do in my blue sportscoat are a pair of stimulant-addled greasers—maybe holdovers still unable to quite make the transition—who have turned the laser beam of considerable charm onto two Japanese teen girls, in private-school uniforms, who clearly speak not a word of English. I spend a few minutes observing this clash of cultures. Then we're heading back up the stairs, taking them two at a time, anxious to get to the next stop.

The crowd is a little older at the Seahorse, which is downstairs and across the street from the newspaper where I once worked. They lounge with studied cool on the threadbare sofas and the long, hacked-up benches, crowd the bar and mill around the pool tables. I buy a round from a passing waiter, shuck and jive my way through the masses. I pass some time in a heated little debate with a couple of rugby players over the gender of the seahorse in the wall aquarium. Then I see him lurching towards me ... Dear God, what the intervening years had wrought: face a road map of deep-cut furrows, scary thousand-mile gaze. He is, I dimly recall, to be avoided at all costs—the type of drunken pain in the ass who always feels compelled to start mouthing off to an AHL hockey thug who has just finished downing a tray of Quevertos. I avert my eyes. He slouches past. But I still feel I've glimpsed the face of Christmas future.

The ship's bell rings, signalling last call. The crowd spills into streets shiny with rain. On the sidewalk a bunch of skinheads wail an old Beatles number with the guitar-playing busker. Next door at the Economy Shoe Shop Café and Bar, the air is heavy with burning Cubanos, they're ordering Glenfiddich and martinis. And everywhere—down Argyle St. towards the octopus of dance spots everyone calls the Liquor Dome and up Blowers St. towards Pizza Corner, the mecca of late-night fast-food cuisine—young hipsters stroll, in twos and threes and in big noisy groups, oblivious to the drizzle tumbling out of a sodden sky, debating where to go next to ensure the party doesn't stop.

I arrange to hook up with John and Jenny later on. First, though, to the Greco-Canadian Social Club, a place frozen in time, far beyond fashionability. Most of the old characters are gone now—the old stevedore known as the Shadow; Billy Carter, the black bootlegger from the North End; Hard Rock Harrigan, the lawyer and piano player; Danny Chisholm, the wild-at-heart bartender. But the game is still going in the corner, the cracked excerpt from a Winston Churchill speech still hangs on the wall, beside the photos of the annual pool tournament winners. The boys are still here. The new Halifax is great, but it is truly wonderful to sit at one of those old Arborite tables hearing the latest stories and catching up on the latest gossip with old friends.

Then on to Birdland, where all roads seem to lead once the Halifax night begins its raucous second act. It bears little resemblance to a place where Charlie Parker might have played, instead being this big industrial bunker where bands with names like the Odds and Ursula thrash away onstage while all around young faces stare in rapt hallucination. The last time I was in this space it catered mostly to the middle-aged divorced, and before that it was a strip club known as the Lobster Trap frequented mainly by navy swabbies. Now I fear I'm probably the only person in the room without a nipple ring. It occurs to me that I probably look to the regular clientele like an ad exec trying to score some dope in the grip of a particularly virulent midlife crisis. The entire room seems devilish, beyond black, the pitiful lights bathed in smoke and sweat, the awful guitar feedback threatening to crush my skull. The dancing is desperate, palsied, as if they all suffered from Tourette's syndrome.

Somewhere along the way I've lost my notebook, which has reduced me to writing on the back of beer coasters and a Blue Rodeo poster I've ripped off the wall. I wad the thing up and jam it into my jacket pocket. The Vietnamese cabbie looks nervous in the rearview.

"To Pier 21," I croak.

Past 1 a. m. now, and Belle and Sam can be merciless little creatures on a morning with a couple of hours' sleep. This is it. One more stop to hook up with my friend Doug who never likes to go to bed and then I'm outta here. Inside the gaping pier the final night of celebration for the enthronement of the new leader of the Shambahla Buddhist community, which settled here in the early 1980s, is going full throttle. But it could be any summer night, really, for Halifax is a festive city now, a place where a general sense of having a good time is shared by all ages, races and levels of wealth and poverty. I don't know who these people are out there roiling on the dance floor to the fiddlers, guitar players and Gaelic singers. A bunch of them, I guess, are Buddhists. Many are just like us, there for the action, spinning, high-stepping and twitching through the closing number. It is "Farewell to Nova Scotia," but a manic, uptempo version of the old standard. When it ends, the final notes bounce and echo through the rafters. Everyone pours out into the night where the air is so moist and salty that a baby could survive in it. Somewhere a buoy clangs and a fog horn wails like a banshee. I need a cab, but none appears. So I just turn my collar up against the damp, take a big breath and start walking between the streetlights that hang like phosphorous ghosts in the night air, leading me home.

Paradise
Is a Personal Thing

—

A DREAM IS MOST OF ALL A SENSUAL EXPERIENCE. YOU MOVE SLOWLY THROUGH it as if under water; events wash over you; strange scenes and unexpected people play at the edge of your vision. Then you awake with only snatches of memory, your heart racing fearfully, an uneasy feeling that something important has happened that you can't put your finger on.

I moved to Ottawa. I went for career, ambition, experience, the usual misguided reasons. A city that runs on juice, power and connections. Pretty, prosperous, way friendlier than I ever expected. But strange in its own way too.

I discovered, for starters, that the temperature is thirty-five above zero in the summer and thirty-five below in the winter. I found that people spent an inordinate amount of time watering their lawns. We moved onto a nice street with friendly people. We skated on the canal, went skiing in the Gatineaus, took the kids to the museums. We found a bar, restaurants, bookstores. Within months, though, I saw the old pattern emerging: drawn to the Halifax papers at the newsstand, ordering six-packs of Keith's at the Beer

Store. Just small things, for sure. But where does it end? At the National Arts Centre, maybe, swaying alongside the rest of the Nova Scotians as the cast of the Cape Breton Summertime Review sings "Out on the Mira." I prayed not.

We had held on to our house in Halifax, which, if not the cottage we'd always wanted, was at least a tangible connection. When vacation time came around we dutifully joined the wagon train east. And when a bunch of families on our street in Ottawa vowed to meet somewhere for a summer road trip I could only smile and say, "Well, I know a place." What I wanted to say was I knew a place where salmon jump, eagles swoop and whales roll. Where pirates and saints and brawlers and believers gather. Where myth, mystery and music hover in the air. Where blunt mountains rise from riverbanks, running out to an ocean that opens to infinity. Where the past and present are interwoven and ineradicable. Where life shimmers with a high-beam vividness.

A couple of years ago I would have started in, the wistful tone in my voice, the misty, far-away look in my eye. Now I knew better. Home, like paradise, is a personal thing. I write these words at a desk in a house one thousand miles away from mine. It is so early that it is still dark outside. But in Nova Scotia the sun is up. Someone is drinking coffee on a front porch. Head tilted hopefully towards the rising light.